SOLAR DESIGN

jovis

Ingrid Hermannsdörfer | Christine Rüb

SOLAR DESIGN

Photovoltaics for Old Buildings, Urban Space, Landscapes
Photovoltaik für Altbau, Stadtraum, Landschaft

jovis

© 2005 by jovis Verlag GmbH

Graphik | Graphics
Barbara Boës, Christine Rüb, Jörg Zeppezauer

Gestaltung und Satz | Design and Setting
Christine Rüb

Bildbearbeitung | Image Editing
Barbara Boës

Übersetzung | Translation
Dieter Bonnet, Katy Derbyshire,
Jörn Frenzel, Ingrid Hermannsdörfer,
Christine O'Donnell, Linda Jayne Turner

Englische Korrektur | English Proofreading
Lynden Cronin, Sam Glück

Beratung | Consultance
Dieter Bonnet

Druck und Bindung | Printing and Binding
GCC Grafisches Centrum Cuno, Calbe

jovis Verlag
Kurfürstenstr. 15/16
10785 Berlin

www.jovis.de

ISBN 3-936314-49-7

Bibliographische Information Der Deutschen Bibliothek
Die Deutsche Bibliothek verzeichnet diese Publikation in der Deutschen Nationalbibliographie; detaillierte bibliographische Daten sind im Internet über http://dnb.ddb.de abrufbar.

Bibliographic information published by Die Deutsche Bibliothek
Die Deutsche Bibliothek lists this publication in the Deutsche Nationalbibliographie; detailed bibliographic data are available in the Internet at http://dnb.ddb.de

Dieses Buch wurde im Rahmen des Forschungsprojektes PVACCEPT mit Fördermitteln der Europäischen Kommission finanziert.

Es enstand im Forschungsschwerpunkt FAKT der Fakultät Gestaltung an der Universität der Künste Berlin.

This book was financed within the research project PVACCEPT by funding of the European Commission.

It was produced at the research centre FACT at the College of Architecture, Media and Design of UdK - Berlin University of the Arts.

Vorwort

Preface

Aktive Sonnenenergienutzung im Baubestand gehört zu den Themen, denen erst in neuerer Zeit mehr Beachtung geschenkt wird. Während die Einbeziehung von Solarstromanlagen (Photovoltaikanlagen) in Neubauten technisch und gestalterisch problemlos möglich ist, bleibt ihre nachträgliche Anwendung im Baubestand häufig aus architektonischer Sicht unbefriedigend. Innovative Ansätze sind erforderlich, um die modernen technologischen Komponenten mit der Maßstäblichkeit, der Farbigkeit, den Materialien und dekorativen Elementen von Altbauten und Denkmälern in Einklang zu bringen.

Die Autorinnen wollen mit diesem Buch an Solararchitektur interessierte Architekten, Fachingenieure, Bauherren, Vertreter von Baubehörden und Gemeindeverwaltungen ansprechen und sie mit neuen gestalterischen Möglichkeiten für den Einsatz von Photovoltaik in den Bereichen Gebäudebestand, Altbauumgebung und Landschaft bekannt machen. Unterschiedliche Anwendungsmöglichkeiten und Konzepte sowie gestalterisch innovative Module werden vorgestellt und durch eine Übersicht über Funktionsweise und Zusammensetzung photovoltaischer Anlagen ergänzt. Den Schwerpunkt des Buches bildet die Darstellung von insgesamt mehr als 30 sehr unterschiedlichen und in hoher ästhetischer Qualität gebauten Beispielen.

Das Buch belegt, wie Solarstromanlagen differenziert und bewusst als bauliche Gestaltungselemente eingesetzt werden können. Es will dazu beitragen, gängige ästhetische Vorbehalte gegenüber der Anbringung von Photovoltaik an Altbauten und denkmalgeschützten Bauten zu entkräften sowie Architekten, Investoren und Denkmalpfleger zu einem entspannten und kreativen Umgang mit dieser umweltfreundlichen Technologie inspirieren.

Ingrid Hermannsdörfer, Christine Rüb

Active use of solar energy in existing buildings has only recently received wider public attention. While the integration of solar power plants (photovoltaic plants) into new buildings is feasible without technical or architectural problems, their supplementary application in existing buildings often leads to solutions which are not satisfactory in architectural terms. Innovative approaches have to be found in order to match the modern technological components to the scale, colour scheme, materials and decorative elements of old buildings and monuments.

In this book the authors want to address architects, engineers, building owners and representatives of planning authorities and public administrations, who are interested in solar architecture. They wish to introduce them to the new design possibilities regarding the use of photovoltaics in existing buildings, in a historic urban context and in natural landscapes. Different possibilities and strategies for photovoltaic applications as well as modules with an innovative design are presented, complemented by information on function and technical composition of photovoltaic plants. As its core theme, the book features more than 30 very different completed projects that meet high aesthetic standards.

The book demonstrates how photovoltaic facilities can be deliberately used as architectural design elements in a highly pronounced way. It aims at reducing common aesthetical reservations against photovoltaic installations on existing buildings and architectural monuments and strives to inspire architects, investors and conservation authorities to adopt a more relaxed and creative attitude towards this environmentally friendly technology.

Ingrid Hermannsdörfer, Christine Rüb

Solare Architektur

Solar Architecture

In den Industriestaaten entfällt durchschnittlich fast die Hälfte des gesamten Energieverbrauchs auf die Energieversorgung von Gebäuden, das heißt auf deren Heizung, Kühlung, Belüftung und Versorgung mit Strom. Immer noch wird die hierfür benötigte Energie weitgehend aus nicht erneuerbaren fossilen Brennstoffen gewonnen, deren Umwandlungsprozesse umweltschädliche Emissionen freisetzen.

Angesichts der begrenzten Verfügbarkeit der fossilen Energieträger und der drohenden und sich teilweise bereits manifestierenden Klimaveränderungen gehören ein rationeller Einsatz und eine effiziente Nutzung von Energie weltweit zu den politischen und gesellschaftlichen Hauptaufgaben. Ein verantwortlicher Umgang mit der Natur und die Nutzung erneuerbarer Energien wie der Solarenergie müssen zur Grundlage auch für die Gestaltung der gebauten Umwelt werden.

Um dieses Ziel zu erreichen, ist ein rasches und gründliches Umdenken derjenigen erforderlich, die am Bau- und Planungsprozess maßgeblich beteiligt sind, also der Architekten, Bauherren und Genehmigungsbehörden. Aber auch der Gesetzgeber ist gefordert, denn neben beruflicher Ausbildung und Finanzierungsmodellen müssen Normen und Gesetze ebenfalls der neuen Zielsetzung angepasst werden. Diese Anpassungsprozesse sind bereits im Gang.

In industrialised countries, on average almost half of the overall energy consumption is apportioned to the energy supply of buildings, that is to heat, cool and ventilate them and supply them with power. The energy required for this still comes from non-renewable fossil fuels and the conversion processes involved release emissions that are harmful to the environment.

In view of the limited availability of fossil energy sources and climate changes that are imminent or already occurring, rational application and efficient use of energy worldwide have become primary political and social aims. A responsible approach to the environment and the use of renewable energies such as solar power must also become a primary consideration when creating the built environment.

In order to achieve this goal, a rapid and thorough rethink is required by those who play a substantial role in the construction and planning process, namely the architects, building owners and regulatory authorities. This also means, among other things, that professional training, models of financing, standard specifications and laws must be adapted to this new objective. These adjustments are already underway.

Gebäude sollten grundsätzlich so gestaltet werden, dass sie möglichst wenig Energie verbrauchen. Dies kann bei Neubauten unter anderem durch entsprechende Ausrichtung (passive Solarenergienutzung) und geeignete Materialwahl (dabei ist möglichst auch auf den Energieverbrauch für die Herstellung zu achten) geschehen. Bei Altbauten kann der Energiebedarf durch Maßnahmen zur Wärmedämmung der Gebäudehülle, Einbau von Fenstern mit besseren Wärmedämmeigenschaften, Austausch von Heizungsanlagen etc. deutlich reduziert werden. Den noch verbleibenden Energiebedarf sollten aktive, Umweltenergie nutzende Systeme decken.

In Deutschland sind ca. 70 Prozent der Bauten älter als 25 Jahre; diese verbrauchen zusammen ungefähr 70 Prozent des Stroms und 95 Prozent der Wärme im Gebäudebereich. Die Instandsetzung und Modernisierung des Gebäudebestandes wird in den nächsten Jahren die Hauptaufgabe für Planer, Architekten und das Baugewerbe darstellen; schon jetzt entfällt die überwiegende Mehrheit der getätigten Baumaßnahmen auf den Altbaubereich. Die Sanierung von Altbauten entscheidet also viel stärker als die Neubauaktivitäten darüber, wie stark der Energieverbrauch durch Gebäude gesenkt werden und wie eine Umstellung auf erneuerbare Energien gelingen kann. Beides ist gleichermaßen wichtig: Die Nutzung regenerativer Energiequellen ist kein Ersatz, sondern eine zeitgemäße Ergänzung zu baulichen Energieeinsparungsmaßnahmen.

Trotzdem wird der Einsatz von erneuerbaren Energien immer noch weitgehend als Aufgabe im Neubaubereich gesehen. Dies betrifft auch die Solararchitektur, da sich thermische und photovoltaische Solaranlagen besonders gut integrieren lassen, wenn sie von Anfang an zusammen mit dem gesamten Gebäude geplant werden. Erst seit kurzem findet eine verstärkte Beschäftigung mit dem Thema der Anpassung von Solaranlagen an bestehende Gebäude statt.

Die 1995 von zahlreichen namhaften Architekten und Architektinnen unterzeichnete „Europäische Charta für Solarenergie in Architektur und Stadtplanung" räumt der umfassenden Nutzung speziell der Solarenergie eine besondere Rolle in der Architektur der Zukunft ein und betont die Bedeutung von Planungs- und Gestaltungskonzepten, welche mit überzeugenden Visualisierungen und Realisierungen zu einer Steigerung der öffentlichen Akzeptanz des solaren Bauens beitragen.

Durch den Einbau einer Solaranlage während der Sanierung eines bestehenden Gebäudes ergeben sich Synergien und Einsparungen, die um so größer sind, je umfassender die Sanierung angelegt ist. Kosteneinsparungen ergeben sich beispielsweise, wenn ein Dach komplett neu gedeckt werden muss und die Solaranlage dort so installiert wird, dass sie Dachziegel einspart, und die installierende Firma gleichzeitig die für die Sanierung ohnehin notwendige Infrastruktur wie Gerüste nutzen kann. Ebenso können Solaranlagen problemlos in geplante Erweiterungsbauten, wie zum Beispiel in Wintergärten, integriert werden.

Grundsätzlich wichtig ist es, Solaranlagen nicht ausschließlich als technologische Systeme zu betrachten, die nur dem Zweck dienen, Wärme oder Strom zu produzieren; vielmehr müssen sie als Elemente angesehen und behandelt werden, die wesentlich zur architektonischen Gestaltung beitragen. So gesehen können sie Architektur aufwerten, akzentuieren, das heißt aus der Masse herausheben; sie können Anpassung und Verwandlung oder Modernität bei gleichzeitiger Bewahrung des Traditionellen ausdrücken oder das „Image" des Gebäudes wie auch seiner Besitzer positiv definieren.

Die Umsetzung solarer Konzepte bei Sanierungen scheitert bislang jedoch häufig an der Schwierigkeit, die modernen technologischen Elemente der Solaranlagen gestalterisch sensibel mit den bestehenden Gebäuden, ihren Dimensionen, Materialien und dekorativen Elementen in Einklang zu bringen. Hier fehlten geeignete Produkte, die eine größere Variabilität der Gestaltung ermöglichen.

An diesem Punkt setzte das deutsch-italienische Forschungs- und Demonstrationsprojekt PVACCEPT ein, das zwischen 2001 und 2004 auf dem Gebiet der Photovoltaik, also dem mit der Stromerzeugung befassten Teil der Solartechnik, innovative Produkte und Gestaltungsmöglichkeiten insbesondere für Altbauten und Gebäude unter Denkmalschutz entwickelte, und dessen Ergebnisse in diesem Buch vorgestellt werden.

Buildings should always be designed so as to use as little energy as possible. In the case of new buildings this can be done through appropriate orientation (passive use of solar energy) and selection of material (paying also as much attention as possible to energy consumption during manufacture). In old buildings energy consumption can be reduced significantly by insulation of the building shell, installation of windows with better insulation characteristics, exchange of heating systems etc. The remaining energy demand should be covered by active systems that use environmental energy.

In Germany, for example, approximately 70 percent of buildings are over 25 years old and together they consume approximately 70 percent of the electricity and 95 percent of the heat in all buildings. Maintenance and renovation measures in existing buildings will present the most common tasks for planners, architects and the building industry in the years to come, given the fact that the vast majority of building activities take place in this sector already. As a result, renovation of old buildings is more decisive than new building activities in determining to what extent energy consumption in buildings can be reduced and how conversion to renewable energies can succeed. Both are equally important: The use of renewable energies is no substitute, but rather a modern complement, to measures which aim at energy saving.

However, the use of renewable energies is currently viewed mainly as a goal within the scope of new buildings. This also includes solar architecture, since solar thermal and photovoltaic facilities can be particularly well integrated if they are planned along with the building as a whole

from the outset. It is only recently that the subject of adapting solar facilities to existing buildings has been increasingly addressed.

The "European Charter for Solar Energy in Architecture and Urban Planning" of 1995, signed by numerous well-known architects, grants the extensive use of solar energy a special role in tomorrow's architecture and emphasises the importance of planning and design concepts that contribute to an increase in public acceptance of the solar building through convincing visualisation and realisation.

The installation of a solar facility during the renovation of an existing building produces synergies and savings that are even greater the more extensive the renovation is. Costs are saved, for example, if a roof has to be completely recovered and a solar facility is installed there, thus saving on tiling and, at the same time, the company carrying out the installation can make use of the infrastructure (e.g. scaffolding) that is required in any case for the renovation. Solar facilities can also be easily integrated into planned extensions such as conservatories.

It is fundamentally important that one does not regard solar facilities as exclusively technological systems that only serve the purpose of producing heat or electricity; instead, they must be regarded and treated as components that make an important contribution to the architectural design. Thus seen, they can enhance the architecture, accentuate it and distinguish it from the mass; they can express adaptation and transformation or modernity while at the same time preserving the traditional features. They can also lend a positive "image" to the building as well as to the owners of the same.

The realisation of solar concepts in renovated buildings has, however, so far frequently failed because of the difficulty in bringing the modern technological components of the solar facilities into line with the existing building, its dimensions, materials and decorative elements in an aesthetically sensitive way. Here there has been a lack of suitable products that would allow for a greater variability of designs.

This was the point of departure for the German-Italian research and demonstration project PVACCEPT, the results of which are presented in this book: Between 2001 and 2004 innovative products and design potentials specifically for old and listed buildings were developed by PVACCEPT in the field of photovoltaics, that is the branch of solar technology dealing with power generation.

PVACCEPT: Das Forschungsprojekt

PVACCEPT: The Research Project

PVACCEPT, ein deutsch-italienisches interdisziplinäres Forschungs- und Demonstrationsvorhaben, ging auf die Initiative einiger Berliner Architektinnen und Architekten im Jahr 2000 zurück, die das komplexe Projekt konzipierten und an der Universität der Künste Berlin verankerten. Von 2001 bis 2004 wurde es von der Europäischen Kommission im 5. Rahmenprogramm unter „Innovation und Förderung der Einbeziehung kleiner und mittlerer Unternehmen" gefördert; zusätzlich trugen die Konsortiumspartner, insbesondere die beteiligten Firmen und Forschungsinstitute, durch erhebliche Eigenanteile zur Finanzierung bei.

PV steht für *photovoltaics*, ACCEPT für *acceptability*. Das Projekt ging von der (später bestätigten) These aus, dass die Gestaltung der Technologie als wichtiger Akzeptanzfaktor bislang erheblich unterschätzt worden sei, und dass besseres und variableres Design der Technologie neue Einsatzmöglichkeiten besonders im Baubestand und an Denkmälern erschließen könne. Entsprechend stand die Entwicklung neuer Gestaltungsansätze im Mittelpunkt der Forschung.

PVACCEPT, an interdisciplinary German-Italian research and demonstration project, arose in the year 2000 thanks to the initiative of a few Berlin architects. They developed the concept and installed the project at the Berlin University of the Arts. From 2001 to 2004 the research was funded by the European Commission within the 5th Framework Programme under "Innovation and the Encouragement of Participation of Small and Medium Enterprises". In addition, the consortium partners, especially the involved companies and research institutes, contributed considerable co-finance.

PV stands for photovoltaics, ACCEPT for acceptability. The project started from the (later confirmed) thesis that the aesthetic design of photovoltaics technology has been considerably underestimated as an important acceptance factor and that improved and more variable design could open new application possibilities, especially in the context of existing buildings and listed monuments. Consequently, the focus of the research was on the development of new design approaches.

Konsortium und Arbeitsteilung

Zusammensetzung des Konsortiums und Arbeitsteilung spiegeln die vielschichtige Projektstruktur wider:

– Die Koordination des Gesamtprojektes und alle anfallenden Entwurfsaufgaben übernahm das Architektenteam an der UdK Berlin (Ingrid Hermannsdörfer, Christine Rüb, Ingo F. Schneider).

– Die Festlegung und Verfolgung interessanter Entwicklungslinien für die innovative Produktgestaltung geschah in enger Zusammenarbeit zwischen den Architekten und den beteiligten Solarfirmen Würth Solar aus Marbach am Neckar und Sunways Photovoltaic Technology aus Konstanz. Durch diese Partner waren unterschiedliche technologische Ansätze vorgegeben: Würth Solar produziert sogenannte CIS-Dünnschichtmodule, Sunways hingegen Solarzellen. Ursprünglich war mit ANTEC Solar aus Arnstadt ein weiterer Produzent von Dünnschichtmodulen (Kadmium-Tellurid-Technologie) beteiligt; die Firma musste das Konsortium jedoch im Jahr 2002 aus unternehmensinternen Gründen verlassen. Damit verblieben die bis dahin mit ANTEC Solar im Rahmen des Projektes entwickelten Produkte in einem frühen Teststadium.

– Das italienische Unternehmen BUSI IMPIANTI aus Bologna, das im Bereich von Planung und Bau kompletter Photovoltaikanlagen tätig ist, übernahm Auslegung und Installation der Demonstrationsvorhaben in Italien und lieferte die nötigen Anlagenkomponenten. Den Bau der deutschen Demonstrationsanlage übernahm Würth Solar.

– Eine wichtige Rolle kam den verschiedenen Akzeptanzstudien zu. Die strukturierten Befragungen von Laien (Bevölkerung) und Experten (Architekten, Vertretern von Genehmigungsbehörden, Lokalpolitikern) in Deutschland und Italien wurden von den Forschungsinstituten IÖW Institut für ökologische Wirtschaftsforschung Berlin und Ambiente Italia Rom durchgeführt. Im ersten Projekthalbjahr lag der Schwerpunkt auf der Frage nach der Bedeutung der Gestaltung für die Akzeptanz von Photovoltaik generell sowie von Installationen an denkmalgeschützten Bauten; nach dem Bau der Demonstrationsanlagen ging es darum, zu ermitteln, wie deren innovative Gestaltung angenommen und bewertet wird. Diese Studien wurden ergänzt durch eine Passantenbefragung anlässlich der öffentlichen Präsentation von ersten Entwurfsideen in Ligurien und eine Befragung von Touristen zu den gebauten Demonstrationsanlagen; diese beiden Untersuchungen wurden vom Architektenteam der UdK Berlin konzipiert und durchgeführt.

– Abgerundet wurde das Projekt durch eine Lebenszyklusanalyse der innovativen Module und Demonstrationsanlagen. Diese Analyse der Energiekreisläufe und Umwelteinflüsse wurde kontinuierlich und parallel zu den Entwicklungsprozessen im Projekt an der Chemiefakultät der Universität Siena durchgeführt.

– Um die Übertragbarkeit der Projektergebnisse zu gewährleisten, wurden europäische Beobachter eingebunden. Ihr kritisches Feedback, vor allem in gemeinsamen Workshops und während der Abschlusskonferenz, war für das Projekt eine wertvolle Unterstützung. Vier europäische Länder waren vertreten:

Frankreich:
– CSTB, Centre Scientifique et Technique du Bâtiment, Paris
– ARMINES, Centre d'Énergétique, École des Mines, Paris

Niederlande:
– IIUE, The International Institute for the Urban Environment, Delft
– EDC, European Design Centre, Eindhoven

Österreich:
– respect, Institut für Integrativen Tourismus und Entwicklung, Wien
– 17&4 Organisationsberatung GmbH, Wien

Spanien:
– AGENER, Agencia de Gestión Energética de la provincia de Jaén, Jaén.

Europäische Komission
European Commission
Förderung
Funding

Universität der Künste Berlin
Koordination + Gestaltung + Planung
Coordination + Design + Planning

Würth Solar GmbH & Co. KG
Modulherstellung
Module Production

sunways
Photovoltaic Technology

Sunways Photovoltaic Technology
Zellherstellung
Cell Production

BUSI IMPIANTI SpA
Bau der Demonstrationsobjekte
Construction of Demonstration Objects

Università degli Studi di Siena
Lebenszyklusanalyse
Life Cycle Assessment

Istituto di Ricerche Ambiente Italia srl
Akzeptanzstudien
Acceptability Studies

Institut für ökologische Wirtschaftsforschung
Akzeptanzstudien
Acceptability Studies

Europäische Beobachter
European Observers
Stellungnahmen zur Übertragbarkeit
Statements on Transferability

Gemeinden und Behörden
Local Councils and Authorities
Zusammenarbeit bei Auswahl und Bau der
Demonstrationsobjekte
Cooperation on Demonstration Objects

Consortium and Division of Labour

The consortium composition and division of labour reflect the complex project structure:

– The overall coordination of the project as well as all tasks on the design level were taken over by the team of architects at UdK Berlin (Ingrid Hermannsdörfer, Christine Rüb, Ingo F. Schneider).

– The architects defined and pursued various innovative approaches to design development in close cooperation with the solar manufacturers Würth Solar from Marbach am Neckar and Sunways Photovoltaic Technology from Konstanz. This choice of partners determined different technological approaches: Würth Solar produces so-called CIS thin-film modules, while Sunways is a producer of solar cells. At the beginning a further producer of thin-film modules (cadmium-telluride technology) was involved – ANTEC Solar from Arnstadt – but had to leave the consortium in 2002 due to internal company reasons. As a consequence the products developed up to then in cooperation with ANTEC Solar did not reach more than an early test stage.

– The Italian company BUSI IMPIANTI from Bologna, active in planning and building complete photovoltaic facilities, was responsible for the technical layout and installation of the demonstration objects in Italy as well as for the delivery of the necessary technical components. The German demonstration object was installed by Würth Solar.

– An important role was ascribed to the different acceptability studies. The structured interviews of laymen (population) and experts (architects, representatives of building permission authorities, politicians) were carried out in Germany and Italy by the research institutes IÖW (Institute for Ecological Economy Research) Berlin and Ambiente Italia Rome. During the first six months of the project their focus was on the importance of design for the acceptability of photovoltaics in general and especially of photovoltaic installations on listed monuments. After the demonstration plants had been constructed, the inquiries aimed at evaluating how their innovative design was accepted and judged. These studies were complemented by random interviews within the frame of an exhibition of first designs for possible demonstration projects in Liguria and a questioning of tourists concerning the built demonstration plants. Both investigations were conceived and carried out by the team of architects at UdK Berlin.

– The project was completed with a life cycle assessment of the innovative modules and installations. This analysis of energy cycles and environmental impacts was carried out continuously, and in parallel to the development processes within the project, at the Faculty of Chemistry at the University of Siena.

– European Observers were involved in crucial stages of the project in order to guarantee that the results would be transferable. Their critical feedback, especially in joint workshops and during the final conference, formed a valuable support base for the research. Four European countries were represented:

France:
– CSTB, Centre Scientifique et Technique du Bâtiment, Paris
– ARMINES, Centre d'Énergétique, École des Mines, Paris

Netherlands:
– IIUE, The International Institute for the Urban Environment, Delft
– EDC, European Design Centre, Eindhoven

Austria:
– respect, Institute for Integrative Tourism and Development, Vienna
– 17&4 Organisational Consulting GmbH, Vienna

Spain:
– AGENER, Energy Agency of the Province of Jaén, Jaén

Produktentwicklung

In enger Kooperation zwischen den Architekten – zeitweise unterstützt von Produktdesignern (Craftsmen Design Berlin) – und den Solarproduzenten wurden verschiedene Entwicklungsrichtungen verfolgt: Semitransparenz von Modulen und Zellen in unterschiedlicher Form, Veränderung der Farbigkeit vor allem durch Oberflächenbedruckung, Erzeugen matter bzw. weniger glänzender Oberflächen sowie Entwurf von multifunktionalen Objekten.

Ziel war die Entwicklung marktfähiger Produkte, die den spezifischen gestalterischen Ansprüchen an die Anwendung bei Altbauten und in der Landschaft entsprechen sollten. Angestrebt wurde ein großes Maß an gestalterischer Flexibilität bei möglichst geringen Eingriffen in den Produktionsprozess. Prototypen sollten in geeigneten Demonstrationsvorhaben zum Einsatz kommen und unter realistischen Bedingungen getestet werden. Diese Kriterien wie auch die Auswahl der Bauvorhaben schränkten die möglichen Modulvarianten ein und erforderten Kompromissbereitschaft bei Designern wie Solarfirmen. Die aus dem Entwicklungsprozess hervorgegangenen Prototypen werden im Kapitel „Innovative Zellen und Module" vorgestellt.

Zusammenarbeit mit Gemeinden und Behörden

Planung und Bau der Demonstrationsanlagen erforderten eine enge Zusammenarbeit zwischen den Architekten des UdK-Teams und den jeweiligen Gemeinden sowie Genehmigungsbehörden, einschließlich der Denkmalpflege. Die Abstimmungsprozesse waren umfangreich und zeitaufwendig, nicht zuletzt wegen der komplexen Kriterien für die Standortauswahl. Die Demonstrationsanlagen sollten sehr sichtbar, also an prägnanten Orten installiert, und im finanziellen und zeitlichen Rahmen des Projektes realisierbar sein. Außerdem sollten sie nicht mit gängigen Photovoltaikmodulen zu realisieren sein, sondern einen innovativen Ansatz und ein hohes Maß an gestalterischer Integration erfordern. Die touristische Nutzung des jeweiligen Objektes war ein weiteres Auswahlkriterium, da dem Tourismus eine Multiplikatorfunktion zugeschrieben wurde. Zusätzlich sollten die gefundenen Lösungen auf andere europäische Länderkontexte übertragbar sein.

Die Demonstrationsanlagen

Als Ergebnis der Zusammenarbeit wurden im Jahr 2004 vier sehr unterschiedliche Demonstrationsanlagen in Süddeutschland und Ligurien (Italien) realisiert, von denen drei sogar an denkmalgeschützten Bauwerken angebracht sind:

– eine Solartafel mit Schillerzitat an der Stadtmauer von Marbach am Neckar, dem Geburtsort Friedrich Schillers
– eine solare Informationstafel an der historischen Festung *San Giorgio* in La Spezia mit Bezug zum dort untergebrachten Museum
– eine Installation von selbstleuchtenden „Solarflaggen" (*solar flags*) im Innenhof der Festungsanlage *Castello Doria* in Porto Venere
– drei solare Pergolen mit semitransparenten Modulen am Yachthafen in der Gemeinde Ameglia, Ortsteil Bocca di Magra.

Die Anlagen werden im Kapitel „Gelungene Praxisbeispiele" vorgestellt und sind dort als PVACCEPT-Demonstrationsanlagen gekennzeichnet.

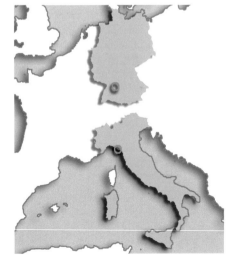

1

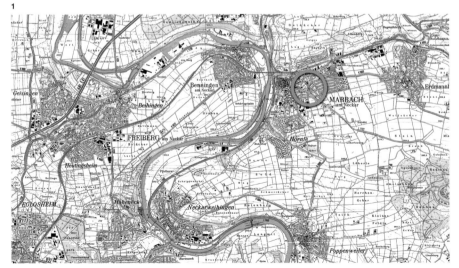

1

Karte mit dem deutschen Demonstrationsstandort
Map indicating the German demonstration site

2

Karte mit den drei Demonstrationsstandorten in Italien
Map indicating the three demonstration sites in Italy

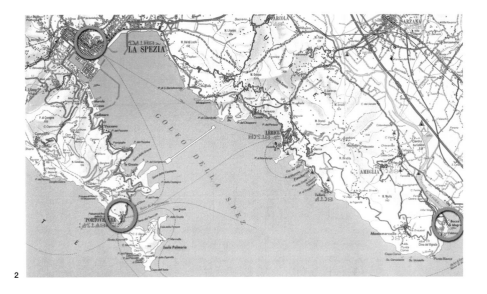

2

Product Development

The research followed different development lines based on a close cooperation between the architects – partly supported by product designers (Craftsmen Design Berlin) – and the solar technology producers: semitransparent modules and cells in varying forms, changes in colour primarily by means of surface printing, the creation of matt and less shiny surfaces and the design of multi-functional objects.

The objective was to develop marketable products which meet the specific design requirements to be considered when photovoltaics are installed at old buildings and in landscapes. They were aimed at providing a high level of design flexibility while at the same time requiring as few changes to the production process as possible. Prototypes were to be applied in appropriate demonstration sites and tested under realistic conditions. These criteria, like the selection of projects, limited the possible module variations and required both the designers and the solar companies to make compromises. The prototypes, which are the result of this joint development process, are presented in more detail in the chapter "Innovative Cells and Modules".

Cooperation with Local Councils and Authorities

Planning and constructing the demonstration plants required close cooperation between the architects of the UdK-team and the town councils and public bodies concerned, including monument protection authorities. The discussions, with the aim of reaching agreements, were extensive and time-consuming, partly as a result of the complex criteria regarding the site selection. The installations were to be installed with a high degree of visibility and had to be feasible within the schedule and financial frame of the project. Sites were sought where the application of standard photovoltaic modules would not be possible and which would therefore require an innovative approach and a high level of aesthetic integration. As tourism was ascribed a multiplier function, the use of the objects for tourism purposes was a further selection criterion. Additionally, the design solutions were to be transferable to the contexts of other European countries.

The Demonstration Plants

In 2004, the project succeeded in implementing four very different demonstration systems in southern Germany and Liguria (Italy), three of which are even mounted on listed buildings:
– A solar board with a quotation by Friedrich Schiller mounted on the city wall of Marbach am Neckar, the birthplace of the German poet
– A solar information panel installed at the historical castle of *San Giorgio* in La Spezia, relating to the museum housed there
– An installation of self-illuminating so-called "solar flags" in the inner courtyard of the *Castello Doria* in Porto Venere
– Three solar pergolas with semitransparent modules, installed at the yacht harbour of Bocca di Magra (municipality of Ameglia).

The installations are described in the chapter "Best Practice Examples" and marked as PVACCEPT demonstration plants.

Ergebnisse der Akzeptanzstudien

Die Ergebnisse der Akzeptanzstudien bestätigten die These von der Bedeutung der Gestaltung für die Akzeptanz, auf der die Forschungsarbeit gründete: Die Hälfte der Ende 2001 in Italien befragten Personen und jeder Zehnte der Befragten in Deutschland gab an, er finde die auf dem Markt befindlichen Standardmodule „nicht ästhetisch"; gleichzeitig waren zwei Drittel der Befragten in Italien und drei Viertel derjenigen in Deutschland der Meinung, die Installation von Photovoltaikanlagen sei „selbst an historischen Gebäuden möglich, wenn die technologischen Elemente gestalterisch entsprechend angepasst wären".

Im September 2004 ergab eine Befragung von Touristen und einheimischer Bevölkerung zu den vier gebauten Demonstrationsanlagen eine hohe Akzeptanz dieser Installationen. Je nach Anlagentyp fanden zwischen 57 und 98 Prozent aller Befragten die jeweilige Anlage „gut integriert", zwischen 77 und 98 Prozent hielten es für „eine gute Idee, Solarmodule in solcher Form zu gestalten", und 54 bis 86 Prozent waren der Meinung, dass „auch an Baudenkmälern Solaranlagen angebracht werden sollten".

Dass die innovativen Module von PVACCEPT unauffällig in ihre Umgebung integriert sind, wurde dadurch bestätigt, dass die *solar flags* von 29 Prozent, die solaren Pergolen von 53 Prozent, die solare Informationstafel am Museum von 62 Prozent und die solare Zitattafel an der Stadtmauer sogar von 84 Prozent der Befragten nicht sofort als Photovoltaikanlagen erkannt wurden.

Zusammenfassung

Auf der Schlusskonferenz in Berlin im November 2004 bestand bei Konsortiumsmitgliedern, Beobachtern und externen Experten Einigkeit darüber, dass nicht nur im Neubaubereich, sondern gerade auch im Gebäudebestand ein erhebliches Potential für die architektonisch sensible Integration von Photovoltaikanlagen vorhanden ist und genutzt werden sollte. Die aus dem Forschungsprojekt hervorgegangenen innovativen Gestaltungsideen und Produkte bieten hier gute Möglichkeiten und Ansätze mit erheblichem Potential für eine Weiterentwicklung. Die Projektergebnisse – auch die ermutigenden Resultate der Lebenszyklusanalyse – legen nahe, dass es sinnvoll und ökonomisch interessant für die Technologieproduzenten ist, sich bei der Neuentwicklung von Photovoltaikprodukten nicht primär nur auf die Steigerung der Energieeffizienz zu konzentrieren, sondern der Bedeutung eines guten Designs als Marketingfaktor mehr Aufmerksamkeit zu schenken. Gestaltung ist ein wesentlicher Verkaufsfaktor für Produkte aller Art; und viele Konsumenten oder Investoren sind bereit, dafür und für das bessere Image, das damit verbunden ist, etwas höhere Kosten in Kauf zu nehmen. Dies bedeutet nicht, dass Design finanzielle Faktoren außer Acht lassen darf; doch eine variablere Gestaltung wird eine entsprechende Nachfrage erzeugen und mit höheren Produktionszahlen auch sinkende Kosten zur Folge haben.

Architekten können bei der weiteren Verbreitung der Technologie als Multiplikatoren betrachtet werden. Ihnen kommt bei der Beratung der Bauherren eine wichtige Rolle als Vermittler zwischen den technischen und energetischen Erfordernissen einerseits und den gestalterischen Ansprüchen andererseits zu.

Ausstellung

Als Informations- und Schulungsmaterial produzierte PVACCEPT eine für unterschiedliche Zielgruppen geeignete Ausstellung. Sie informiert über Anwendungsfelder für Photovoltaik in den Bereichen Altbau, Stadtraum und Landschaft und stellt neue Gestaltungsmöglichkeiten mit Photovoltaik sowie die wichtigsten technischen Hintergründe kurz vor. Die Ausstellung ist in den Sprachen Deutsch, Englisch und Italienisch erhältlich und kann von interessierten Institutionen, wie zum Beispiel Stadtverwaltungen, Architekten- und Handwerkskammern oder Bildungseinrichtungen, ausgeliehen werden. Nähere Informationen dazu finden sich auf der Projekt-Homepage unter www.pvaccept.de.

Results of the Acceptability Studies

The findings of the studies confirmed the main thesis, regarding the significance of design for acceptability, on which the research work was based: Half of those interviewed in Italy at the end of 2001 and every tenth interviewee in Germany stated that they found the standard modules available on the market "not aesthetically pleasing". At the same time, two thirds of the interviewees in Italy and three quarters of those interviewed in Germany expressed the opinion that installing photovoltaics was "even possible on historical buildings, if the design of the technological elements was suitably adapted".

A survey conducted among tourists and the local population in September 2004, on the four demonstration facilities constructed, showed a high degree of acceptance for these installations. Depending on the type of equipment, between 57 and 98 percent of all interviewees found the installation in question "well integrated", between 77 and 98 percent thought it was "a good idea to design solar modules in such a form" and 54 to 86 percent agreed that "solar equipment should also be installed on listed buildings".

The fact that the innovative modules, which were developed and applied by PVACCEPT, are very inconspicuous was, as such, confirmed by the survey: 29 percent of the interviewees did not immediately recognise the "solar flags" as photovoltaic facilities; 62 percent failed to identify the solar information panel on the museum, 84 percent the solar quotation board on the city wall and 53 percent the solar pergolas as photovoltaic installations.

Summary

The participants of the final conference held in Berlin in November 2004 – consortium members, European observers and external experts – conclusively agreed that there is considerable potential for integrating photovoltaics in an architecturally sensitive manner, not just in the field of new construction, but also in existing buildings, and that this potential should be exploited. The innovative design ideas and products developed by PVACCEPT offer good opportunities and approaches that can be further pursued.

The outcomes of the project – including the encouraging results of the life cycle assessment – may encourage technology producers to consider it as useful, and within their economic interests, to shift the focus in photovoltaic product development away from only increasing energy efficiency and to pay more attention to good design as a marketing factor. Aesthetic design is an essential factor for selling products of all kinds and many consumers and investors are willing to pay a little more for better design and the positive image coupled with it. This does not mean that design can neglect financial aspects; but more design variability will create a corresponding demand and cost decreases will be the result of rising production figures.

Architects can be regarded as multipliers for the further dissemination of the technology. They play an important role as the advisors of clients, intermediating between the technical and energy-related requirements on the one hand and the architectural and aesthetic demands on the other.

Exhibition

PVACCEPT has produced an exhibition as information and training material. This provides information on the application of photovoltaics in the context of old buildings, urban space and landscapes and shows new design possibilities with photovoltaics, in addition to their technical backgrounds. The exhibition is available in the following languages: German, English and Italian. Any interested institutions, for example city administrations, chambers of architects, chambers of crafts and educational institutions can hire it. More information can be found on the project homepage: www.pvaccept.de.

Simulation von „Ziegelmodulen"
am Marstall in Putbus / Deutschland
Simulation of "brick modules"
at the Marstall building in Putbus / Germany

Anwendungsfelder

Range of Applications

Bei Altbauten sind, wie im Neubau, vielfältige Möglichkeiten zur Anbringung von Photovoltaikanlagen gegeben. Die Installationen werden hier jedoch zwangsläufig eher kleinteilig ausfallen, weil sie auf existierende Strukturen Rücksicht nehmen müssen. Außerdem sind Standardlösungen oft nicht einsetzbar, so dass innovative Ansätze gefragt sind. Dies betrifft die Gestaltung der Module selbst, aber auch zum Beispiel den Entwurf geeigneter Trag- und Unterkonstruktionen. Insbesondere gilt dies bei denkmalgeschützten Gebäuden, bei denen die technischen Eingriffe in die vorhandene Bausubstanz minimal gehalten werden müssen. Auch bei der Installation von Photovoltaikanlagen in der Landschaft sind innovative Ansätze erforderlich, vor allem bezüglich der Farbigkeit der Module und ihrer Anpassung an vorhandene natürliche Strukturen. Während es in den Bereichen Altbau, Denkmäler und Landschaft überwiegend darum geht, die technologischen Elemente sensibel an ihre Umgebung anzupassen, erfordert die Photovoltaikanwendung im Stadtraum eher die Auseinandersetzung mit Multifunktionalität bzw. mit der Erschließung zusätzlicher Funktionen.

Im Folgenden werden die unterschiedlichen Anwendungsfelder im Überblick kurz dargestellt. Der Schwerpunkt liegt dabei auf gestalterischen und grundsätzlichen Aspekten. Eine Auseinandersetzung mit konstruktiven Details kann an dieser Stelle nicht stattfinden: In den angesprochenen Bereichen muss, anders als im Neubau, immer die individuelle, vorgefundene Situation im Mittelpunkt des Entwurfs stehen, weshalb sich Gestaltung und Konstruktion hier nicht standardisieren lassen.

Existing or historic buildings, like new buildings, present a broad range of possibilities for photovoltaic applications. However, installations on existing buildings unavoidably tend to be more fragmented than on new buildings, since they have to comply with an existing context. As standardised products are often not applicable, the situation calls for innovative approaches. This concerns the design of the modules themselves, but also, for example, the design of appropriate sub-structures. In particular this applies to listed buildings, given the fact that technical interventions into their structures have to be minimised. Innovative approaches are also required when constructing photovoltaic facilities in rural or park areas; above all, this concerns the colour scheme of the modules and their adaptation to the existing natural environment. While existing buildings, monuments and landscapes mainly call for a subtle integration of the technological components into the given context, the focus concerning photovoltaic installations in urban space is more on multiple, respectively new additional functions.

The following chapter provides a brief summary of the range of possible applications, emphasizing design-related and general aspects. It does not refer to structural details, because the architectural design with regard to the aforementioned application fields – as opposed to new buildings – has to be derived from the individual situation. Hence, the resulting design and structure cannot follow a standardised pattern.

Photovoltaik auf Dächern

Zunächst eignen sich natürlich Dachflächen für die Photovoltaikinstallation, und zwar Flachdächer ebenso wie geneigte Dächer aufgrund ihrer meist unverschatteten Lage. Im Altbaubereich liegen hier noch große Nutzungspotentiale brach.

Flachdächer sind eine gute Option für die Aufstellung von Photovoltaikanlagen: Die Module können in solartechnisch idealer Ausrichtung und Neigung auf oft großen zusammenhängenden Flächen errichtet werden, Montage und Wartung sind ohne Hilfsmittel wie Baugerüste möglich. Solaranlagen auf Flachdächern sind bei höheren Gebäuden wenig sichtbar und können deshalb problemlos auch mit Standardmodulen ausgeführt werden. Eine sinnvolle Alternative für genutzte Dachterrassenflächen ist ein Wetterschutz in Form einer solaren Pergola.

Anlagen auf geneigten Dächern versprechen in geeigneter Ausrichtung ebenfalls eine gute Energieausbeute. Zahlreiche auf dem Markt erhältliche Modultypen stehen für die Auf-Dach- ebenso wie die In-Dach-Montage zur Verfügung. Das zusätzliche Konstruktionsgewicht bei der Auf-Dach-Montage erfordert im Normalfall keine statischen Veränderungen am vorhandenen Dachstuhl.

Aber auch gewölbte Dächer, zum Beispiel Tonnendächer, können mit Photovoltaik ausgestattet werden – unter der Voraussetzung, dass die Modulgrößen angepasst bzw. verringert werden, um der Krümmung zu folgen. Es gibt auch die Alternative, flexible Solarzellen in gekrümmte Module einzubetten; in diesem Fall sind keine speziellen Einschränkungen bezüglich der Größen zu beachten. Allerdings gibt es im Hinblick auf die sonstigen technologischen Anlagenkomponenten (zum Beispiel Wechselrichter) gewisse Idealgrößen.

Bei unregelmäßigen und somit verschatteten Dachflächen, geringem Energiebedarf oder in Fällen, in denen aus ästhetischen Gründen größere zusammenhängende Modulflächen nicht erwünscht sind, können auch kleinere Flächen, beispielsweise an Schornsteinen oder auf Dachgauben, genutzt werden. Unter gestalterischen Gesichtspunkten sind Schleppgauben hierfür besser geeignet als andere Gaubenformen, da ihre Dachfläche nur nach einer Seite ausgerichtet ist.

Generell sollten sich die individuelle Konstruktion und Gestaltung der Photovoltaikanlage an Form, Farbe und Material des vorhandenen Dachs orientieren.

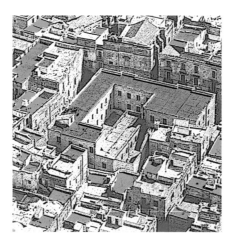 

Schematische Darstellung von Flächen, die sich für eine Photovoltaikinstallation eignen

Due to their mostly unshaded position, roof areas are well suited for the installation of photovoltaics in the first place. This applies to pitched roofs and flat roofs alike. In this context, existing buildings still offer a great potential for further development.

Flat roofs are a good option: They often provide large connected surface areas and the orientation and inclination of the modules can be optimised according to the technological requirements. Furthermore, installation and maintenance are possible without the need for scaffolding. Solar facilities on flat roofs of reasonably high buildings are almost completely indistinguishable from below and can therefore be composed of standard "off-the-shelf" products without problems. A practical alternative is provided by solar pergolas, which can function as weather protection above roof terraces.

Photovoltaic facilities on pitched roofs, when facing in the right direction, also promise good energy yields. A broad range of products are available on the market for roof-attached as well as roof-integrated systems. Usually, the additional weight of externally attached photovoltaic modules does not make structural alterations to the roof necessary.

Photovoltaics may even be installed on domed roofs (for example barrel roofs), on condition that the module sizes are adapted (i.e. reduced) to shape the curve. Alternatively, flexible solar cells can be imbedded into curved modules; this does not entail any particular limitations concerning sizes. However, there are optimum sizes with respect to some other technological components of photovoltaic installations (for instance inverters).

In cases of irregular and thus shaded roof surfaces, low energy requirements, or if large-scale module surfaces are not desirable for aesthetic reasons, smaller surfaces such as on chimneys or dormers can also be used. From an architectural point of view, shed dormers are better suited than other types, as their roof areas face in only one direction.

In general, the individual structure and architectural design of the photovoltaic facility should be derived from the shape, colour and material of the existing roof.

Schematic illustration of surfaces suitable for photovoltaic installation

Photovoltaik an Fassaden

Auch Fassadenflächen in ihrer Vielfalt eignen sich für die Integration von Photovoltaik. Eine vertikale Anbringung von Photovoltaikmodulen bringt zwar eine geringere Energieeffizienz mit sich als die Montage auf schrägen Flächen; trotzdem ist beispielsweise bei (partiell) verschatteten oder nicht nach Süden, Südosten oder Südwesten ausgerichteten Dachflächen eine südorientierte Fassadeninstallation oftmals die effektivere Lösung.

Je nach Baualter und Architektur ist die Photovoltaikinstallation an bestehenden Fassaden unterschiedlich kompliziert. Bei Gebäuden in Betonskelettbauweise mit vorgehängter Fassade, wie sie sich nach dem Zweiten Weltkrieg etablierte, ist eine nachträgliche Photovoltaikintegration in die Fassade meist unkompliziert zu realisieren. Schwierig ist die photovoltaische Nachrüstung von Gebäuden der vorindustriellen Epochen, deren Wände in Massivbauweise aus Mauerwerk mit Putz oder als Fachwerk hergestellt sind. In diesen Fällen entsprechen die Maßsysteme des Bauwerks häufig nicht den Maßen der Standardmodule, so dass individuell angepasste Lösungen zum Einsatz kommen müssen.

Je nach Baustil (analog zum Gebäudealter) und Planungsaspekt (von vorneherein integriert oder nachträglich angebracht) kann eine Fassadengestaltung mit Photovoltaik großflächig oder eher kleinteilig ausfallen. Für eine großflächige Anbringung sind beispielsweise Brandwände geeignet, für eine kleinteilige Nutzung unter anderem Brüstungen, Flächen zwischen Fenstern, aber auch Gesimse, Schiebetüren und Laubengänge. Insbesondere Elemente, die als Wetter-, Sicht- und Sonnenschutz genutzt werden, wie Fensterläden, Vordächer und Loggien, bieten sich für die Photovoltaikinstallation an. Für viele Fassadenanwendungen stellen entsprechend semitransparente Module eine gute Lösung dar. Wenn sie in Fensterflächen integriert werden, können sie auch die Funktion eines Sonnenschutzes mit übernehmen.

Schematische Darstellung von Flächen, die sich für eine Photovoltaikinstallation eignen

Façade surfaces, in their diversity, are also suited to the integration of photovoltaics. It has to be taken into consideration that the vertical installation of solar panels is less energy efficient than installation on inclined surfaces; nevertheless, a south-facing façade installation may still prove to be more efficient than modules on a roof that is (partly) shaded or that does not face towards the south, southeast or southwest directions.

The complexity of installing photovoltaics onto an existing façade varies, depending on the age and architecture of the building. With regard to the curtain-walled, framed concrete constructions of the post-war era, retrofitting photovoltaics onto the façades is a mostly uncomplicated process. The scenario is more difficult in the case of pre-industrial buildings with rendered masonry walls or timber-framed structures. In these cases the respective historical modular systems of the building often do not correspond with the dimensions of standard photovoltaic modules. Hence, special tailored solutions have to be applied.

Depending on the style (analogously to the age) of the building and the planning aspect (integrated from the beginning or attached later on), a façade design incorporating photovoltaics may result in large-scale or rather fragmented compositions. Compartment walls, for example, lend themselves well to large-scale applications, whereas balustrades, spaces between windows, cornices, sliding doors and access galleries, among others, are suitable for fragmented applications. Building elements, especially those that provide weather, sun or eyesight protection, such as window shutters, canopies and loggias, also lend themselves to the application of photovoltaics. Semitransparent modules provide good solutions in this context. By integrating them into windows they can assume an additional function as solar shading.

Schematic illustration of surfaces suitable for photovoltaic installation

Photovoltaik im Stadtraum

Im öffentlichen Raum tritt Photovoltaik bereits zunehmend in Erscheinung, beispielsweise als Energiequelle für Parkscheinautomaten. Die Nutzungsmöglichkeiten werden jedoch längst nicht ausgeschöpft; gerade im Bereich der sogenannten Straßenmöbel liegen hier noch beträchtliche Potentiale. Multifunktionale Kombinationen aus Photovoltaikelementen und mit modernen, Energie sparenden Leuchtdioden ausgestatteten Lampen, die mit dem solar erzeugten Strom gespeist werden, sind nur eine Möglichkeit.

So lassen sich mit Solarmodulen besonders gut alle möglichen Arten von Überdachungen gestalten, zum Beispiel an Bushaltestellen oder städtischen Plätzen. In diese Kategorie fallen auch solare Pergolen, die mehrere Funktionen von Sonnenschutz bis Sitzgelegenheit kombinieren können.

Breite Anwendungsmöglichkeiten bieten auch Funktionen im Zusammenhang mit Information, Kommunikation und Transport. Solare Informationstafeln beispielsweise könnten immer mehr zum Standard werden, statt wie bisher noch die Ausnahme zu sein.

Lärmschutzwände an viel befahrenen Straßen bieten sich ebenfalls für die Integration von Photovoltaik an; der erzeugte Strom könnte gleich an Ort und Stelle für die Straßenbeleuchtung eingesetzt werden.

Das Konzept von integrierten Anwendungsszenarien geht noch darüber hinaus und könnte in seiner Umsetzung dazu beitragen, langfristig die Ziele einer grundsätzlich nachhaltigen städtischen Entwicklung, einer umweltfreundlichen Energieversorgung und eines „sanften" Tourismus zu unterstützen: Am solaren Schalter wird das Ticket für die Solarfähre gekauft, unter der solaren Pergola gibt es einen Verleih und eine Solartankstelle für umweltfreundliche Elektrofahrzeuge usw.

Selbst der Bereich der Kunst im Stadtraum (wie auch in der Landschaft) bietet interessante Möglichkeiten für die Objektgestaltung mit Photovoltaik. Es gibt bereits an verschiedenen Standorten solare Kunstobjekte unterschiedlichster Art, die, wie auch die solaren Straßenmöbel, wesentlich dazu beitragen können, diese umweltfreundliche Technologie populärer zu machen.

Schematische Darstellung von Flächen, die sich für eine Photovoltaikinstallation eignen

Photovoltaic installations are in the process of becoming more visible in public space, for instance as an energy source for parking ticket machines. The potential of photovoltaic applications in public space is, however, not being fully utilised; this is particularly the case in the sector of so-called "street furniture". Multi-functional combinations of photovoltaic elements with lamps, equipped with modern energy-saving light emitting diodes (LEDs), are only one of the many possibilities for the use of photovoltaics in street furniture.

Photovoltaic modules are also highly suitable for all kinds of roofs and shelters, ranging from bus stops to canopies over urban squares. Multi-functional solar pergolas, which can assume hybrid functions ranging from sun protection to seating, also fit into this category.

Further fields offering a broad spectrum of potential applications are those connected with information, communication and transport. Solar information boards, for example, could become a norm rather than an exception, as is the case today.

Noise barriers alongside busy roads are also well suited for the integration of photovoltaics; the generated energy might be used on the spot to power adjacent street lighting.

The concept of integrated application scenarios goes even further than that and could, once realized, contribute to the achievement of objectives such as a generally sustainable urban development, an environmentally friendly energy supply and a "soft" tourism in the long term: The solar-powered counter sells tickets for the solar ferry, under the solar pergola there is a rental station and a solar fuelling station for electro vehicles etc.

Even the field of art in urban space (as in landscapes) offers interesting possibilities for the design of photovoltaic objects. Works of solar art already exist in different locations and, like solar street furniture, can help to make this environmentally friendly technology more popular.

Schematic illustration of surfaces and objects suitable for photovoltaic installation

Photovoltaik in der Landschaft

Wenn größere Photovoltaikanlagen isoliert in der Landschaft errichtet werden, wird bislang meist mehr Wert auf einen möglichst großen Energieertrag gelegt als auf eine gestalterisch sensible Integration in die Umgebung. Die entsprechend auffälligen Anlagen werden von der Bevölkerung oft als Landschaftszerstörung gesehen und fördern damit nicht die Akzeptanz der Technologie. Mit Phantasie und innovativen Gestaltungsansätzen ist es durchaus möglich, Photovoltaikmodule unauffälliger in die Landschaft, selbst in die von Parks oder Naturschutzgebieten, zu integrieren.

Eine Möglichkeit besteht beispielsweise darin, die Photovoltaik mit schon vorhandenen landschaftsfremden Elementen, etwa Lärmschutzwänden an Autobahnen, Stützwänden oder Wirtschaftsgebäuden wie Scheunen, zu kombinieren. Im besten Fall profitieren diese Elemente sogar gestalterisch von der Photovoltaikintegration.

Eine andere Möglichkeit für eine bessere, das heißt unauffälligere Landschaftsintegration von Photovoltaik besteht darin, natürliche Elemente wie Waldkanten, Hecken oder Bäume zu „imitieren". So wurden bereits an mehreren Orten Varianten von „Solarbäumen" für den

öffentlichen Raum entwickelt, die auch in der Landschaft ihren Platz finden können.

Ein grundsätzliches Problem bei der Landschaftsintegration stellt die übliche Farbigkeit der Module (Dunkelblau oder Schwarz) dar. Diese Farben kommen in der natürlichen Landschaft nicht vor und wirken darin deshalb immer auffällig bzw. fremd. Es gibt jedoch durchaus verschiedene Möglichkeiten zur Herstellung von Modulen in Braun- oder Grüntönen, um diesen Kontrast aufzulösen.

Unabhängig davon, welche Form und welches Design eine Photovoltaikinstallation in der freien Landschaft hat, sind einige Aspekte bei der Planung und Gestaltung besonders zu berücksichtigen: Die Anlagen sollten in irgendeiner Weise gegen Beschädigungen, beispielsweise durch Tiere, aber auch durch Vandalismus oder Diebstahl, geschützt werden. Dies sollte schon bei der Standortwahl berücksichtigt werden, das heißt Standorte, die weniger abgelegen und deshalb auch mehr einer allgemeinen sozialen Kontrolle unterworfen sind, eignen sich besser als sehr abgelegene Orte. Zusätzlich sollte man darauf achten, Unterkonstruktionen zu verwenden, die ein Besteigen der Anlagen verhindern.

Schematische Darstellung von Flächen und Objekten, die sich für eine Photovoltaikinstallation eignen

When large photovoltaic plants are constructed as isolated installations in a landscape, the focus is usually more on achieving the highest energy yield than on the aesthetically sensitive integration of the facility into its natural surroundings. As a consequence, these installations are highly conspicuous and often regarded by the public as being destructive to the landscape, thus not advancing the acceptance of the technology. However, when applying an imaginative and innovative design approach it is possible to integrate photovoltaic modules more inconspicuously into landscapes, even into parks or natural reserves.

One possible approach is, for example, to attach photovoltaic modules to objects, which are alien to the landscape and exist there already, such as noise barriers along motorways, retention walls or agricultural buildings like barns. Ideally, the appearance of these objects will even benefit from the integration of photovoltaics.

Another possibility for better, more subtle landscape integration is to "imitate" natural features like forest edges, hedges or trees. So-called "solar trees", developed already for several urban locations, could also find a place in the rural landscape.

When it comes to the landscape integration of photovoltaics, the standard colour range of modules (dark blue or black) presents a general problem. These colours are not found in natural landscapes and therefore always appear striking or strange in such environments. Yet there are different possibilities of generating modules in shades of brown and green, which may succeed in dissolving this contrast.

Independent from the form and design of a photovoltaic installation in a natural environment, a number of general aspects have to be taken into consideration during the planning stages: The facilities should be protected in some way against damage, for example by animals, but also by vandalism or theft. This should already be taken into account in the choice of the location: Sites which are less isolated and therefore more under the control of the general public, are more appropriate than highly remote locations. Additionally, substructures should be used that prevent people from climbing the facility.

Schematic illustration of surfaces and objects suitable for photovoltaic installation

Gestaltung und Konstruktion

Architectural Design and Construction

Die Photovoltaikinstallation im Bestand, sei es als Komponente einer Sanierung oder eines Neubaus bei einer Baulückenschließung, erfordert von allen Beteiligten einen anspruchsvollen Umgang mit der Thematik. Grundsätzlich sollten Photovoltaikmodule nicht nur als monofunktionale technologische Objekte, sondern als Gestaltungselemente begriffen werden.

Dies gilt auch für Baudenkmäler, bei denen bislang die Installation von Photovoltaik von den Eigentümern wie auch von den Denkmalpflegern selten in Betracht gezogen wird, auch wenn eine Modernisierung der Gebäudetechnik für die weitere Nutzung des Bauwerks ohnehin notwendig ist. Schon im Vorfeld der Sanierungsmaßnahmen sollte deshalb der Dialog mit der zuständigen Denkmalpflegebehörde gesucht werden, damit unterschiedliche Ansätze diskutiert, geprüft und abgestimmt werden können.

Der Planer hat bei Sanierung und Modernisierung einen umfangreichen Katalog von Kriterien zu beurteilen: Die Analyse des Bauwerks bzw. der Umgebung umfasst nicht nur die gestalterische, morphologische und historische Charakteristik, sondern auch die Nutzung und damit verbunden die Anforderungen an Raumkomfort und Energieversorgung. Daraus ergeben sich Art und Umfang der Maßnahmen und die zu erwartenden Kosten. Bei der Planung einer Photovoltaikanlage müssen grundsätzlich drei Ebenen betrachtet werden: Energietechnik, Gestaltung und Konstruktion.

The installation of a photovoltaic system in an existing building context, whether as part of renovation work on an old building or in a new building being erected on a vacant lot, requires the close attention of all parties involved.

Essentially, photovoltaic modules should not be regarded as mere mono-functional technological objects, but as elements of design.

This also applies to listed buildings, where the installation of photovoltaics is seldom being considered by building owners or monument protection authorities, despite the fact that a modernisation of the technical services is necessary for further use of these buildings. It is therefore advisable for the architect, at the earliest stages of a renovation project, to establish close contact with the relevant conservation authorities in order to discuss, check and coordinate various options.

The architect in charge of a renovation and refurbishment project must take many factors into consideration: The analysis of a building or its context is not limited to aesthetic, morphological and historical aspects, but also includes the function of the building and the requirements in terms of room climate and energy supply resulting from it. This will determine the nature and extent of the works and the costs to be expected. Basically, the design of a photovoltaic installation has to take three different aspects into account: Energy engineering, architectural design and structure.

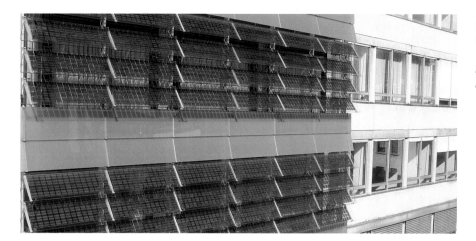

Energietechnik

Die energetische Altbausanierung ist Teil der Gesamtkonzeption für den Erhalt der Bausubstanz und die Wiederherstellung des Erscheinungsbildes eines Gebäudes. Sie ist in der Regel eine Modernisierung verschiedener Bauteile und kann unter anderem Maßnahmen wie die Dämmung der Außenhaut (Fassade und Dach), passiven Energiegewinn durch größere, hochwertig isolierte Fenster sowie den Einsatz sparsamerer Verbraucher (Elektrogeräte, Lampen) umfassen. Zusätzlich kann dabei der Wechsel zu einer umweltfreundlichen Warmwasser- und Stromerzeugung durch Solarkollektoren und -module erfolgen.

Die Entscheidung für Art (an das Stromnetz angeschlossen oder als autarkes „Inselsystem") und Auslegung einer Photovoltaikanlage muss auf der Grundlage von Faktoren wie Klima, Standort und Gebäudenutzung getroffen werden (vgl. hierzu die detaillierte Darstellung im Kapitel „Technische Grundlagen").

Gestaltung

Ziel einer architektonischen Auseinandersetzung im Baubestand ist immer die Orientierung am historischen Bild des Bauwerks. Bei der Installation einer Photovoltaikanlage können im Wesentlichen drei unterschiedliche Ansätze der Gestaltung verfolgt werden:

– Opposition zum Vorhandenen als eigenständiges, souveränes Hinzufügen einer weiteren, durchaus kontrastierenden Schicht
– Dialog als gestalterische Neuinterpretation und Weiterentwicklung des Vorhandenen
– Wiederherstellung und unauffällige Verbindung des Bestandes mit den neuen, modernen Elementen.

Opposition und Kontrast im Sinn der Differenz, nicht der Dissonanz, lassen eine große Bandbreite der Photovoltaikinstallation zu. Gerade mit technologischen Elementen wie der Photovoltaik kann das Prinzip der deutlichen Trennung von Alt und Neu durch Verwendung konträrer Materialien umgesetzt werden.

Photovoltaikinstallation als Neuinterpretation und Dialog respektiert das Vorhandene und antwortet gestalterisch auf dessen Charakter und Eigenart. In vielen Fällen ist hierfür ein Variieren der Modulgrößen notwendig, um bei Dach- wie Fassadenintegrationen auf Rasterung und Flächigkeit der vorhandenen Bauteile und Materialien eingehen zu können.

Die unauffällige Verbindung mit dem Bauwerk, das harmonische Hinzufügen, erfordert noch weitere Anpassung der technologischen Elemente an den Bestand: Oberflächenstruktur, Textur und Farbigkeit sind zusätzliche charakteristische Erscheinungsmerkmale, die zu berücksichtigen sind.

Konstruktion

Konstruktiv lässt sich die Installation von Photovoltaik als Applikation, Addition oder Integration qualifizieren, die Übergänge sind jedoch fließend.

Unter Applikation ist das reversible Anbringen als weiteres Element vor der Gebäudehülle zu verstehen. Sie wird in vielen Fällen der nachträglichen Installation ohne weitere Sanierungsmaßnahmen angewendet. Mit entsprechender Konstruktion wird nur minimal in die Gebäudehülle eingegriffen, ein Rückbau ist spurlos möglich. Bei denkmalgeschützten Gebäuden ist Applikation oftmals die einzige überzeugende Möglichkeit, der Forderung der Genehmigungsbehörden nach minimalen Eingriffen in die Gebäudesubstanz zu entsprechen.

Bei der Addition bilden die Photovoltaikelemente die äußerste Schicht der Gebäudehülle und übernehmen teilweise deren Aufgaben; eine Demontage der Module ohne Ersatz wäre entsprechend nicht möglich. Der Addition liegt also immer ein multifunktionales Bauteil zugrunde. Dieses kann vor Fenstern als Sonnenschutz angebracht sein, kann Wetterschutz über dem Hauseingang und Sichtschutz bei Brüstungen bieten. Um den Energieertrag eines solaren Sonnenschutzes ebenso zu optimieren wie die Verschattung der Innenräume, kann ein nachgeführtes System gewählt werden, bei dem

Energy Engineering

The energy-conscious rehabilitation of an old building is part of the general strategy aimed at preserving the constitution of the building and restoring its original appearance. This process normally involves the alteration of individual building components and may include measures such as the insulation of the building shell (façade and roof), the application of passive energy principles by means of larger, highly insulated windows and the use of low energy appliances. Additionally, the client may opt for a new environmentally friendly system for hot water and power supply based on solar collectors and modules.

The choice of power system (either grid-connected or independent) and the size of the photovoltaic installation must be based on factors such as local climate, location and use of the building. (For a more detailed account of this topic refer to the chapter "Technical Basics".)

Architectural Design

When dealing with an existing building in architectural terms, the objective is always to refer to its historical appearance. Essentially, the installation of a photovoltaic facility can be based on three different design approaches:

– Opposition between old and new elements, the latter being introduced consciously as an independent layer
– Dialogue with and contrast to the existing structure by re-inventing and developing it
– Restoration of the original appearance and inconspicuous blend with the new, modern elements.

Opposition and contrast, here implying difference rather than dissonance, make a broad spectrum of photovoltaic applications possible. Highly technological components, such as solar panels, are particularly well suited to highlighting the difference between old and new through the use of contrasting materials.

Photovoltaic installations that engage in a kind of dialogue with the existing situation respect the original state while at the same time offering a creative re-interpretation of its nature and specifics. In many cases this will involve varying the panel sizes in order to adapt to the grids and shapes of the existing roofs and façades.

Further fine-tuning of the technological elements is required to reach an inconspicuous blend of old and new components and a harmonious integration with the existing building. In this context, surface structure, texture and colour tones are essential visual characteristics to be considered.

Construction

In constructional terms, the installation of photovoltaics can be divided in three categories: Attachment, addition and integration. However, all three categories blend smoothly into each other.

Attachment of photovoltaics denotes the reversible attachment of solar panels, as an additional element, in front of the outer shell of the building. This method is frequently applied when equipping buildings without the need for further renovation. Provided that an appropriate sub-structure is used, fixing as well as the subsequent dismantling of the solar panels is possible with minimum impact on the building. In the case of listed monuments, such attachment will often represent the only application method which convincingly meets the requirements of the building permission authorities for minimal intervention.

The addition of solar panels means that they form the exterior layer of the building shell, assuming some of its functions. In such cases dismantling the panels without replacing them would be impossible. The photovoltaic panels represent here multi-purpose building elements. They may serve as solar protection in front of windows, as a canopy above the main entrance or provide visual protection in balustrades.

Photovoltaische Dachintegration
in Hellerau / Deutschland

Photovoltaic roof integration
in Hellerau / Germany

die Module durch elektromechanisches Drehen dem im Tages- und Jahresrhythmus unterschiedlichen Sonnenstand angepasst werden. Hinterlüftete Photovoltaikfassaden stellen eine gute multifunktionale Alternative zu den häufig verwendeten Natursteinfassaden dar und können ebenso gut wie diese auch repräsentativen Zwecken dienen.

Unter Integration ist der Einbau von Modulen als vollwertiger Bestandteil der Gebäudehülle zu verstehen, deren Aufgaben sie vollständig erfüllen. Integration von Photovoltaik setzt in vielen Fällen Systementwicklung voraus: beispielsweise von Verbundelementen, die alle Aufgaben der Dachhaut erfüllen, sei es als kleinteilige Kaltdachdeckungen oder großformatiges Warmdachelement. Andere Lösungen stellen in Isolierglas eingebettete Solarzellen als Blend- und Sichtschutz dar, oder auch solare Doppelfassaden; bei letzteren kann der erzeugte Strom im Sommer zur Klimatisierung genutzt werden, während im Winter die Stauwärme zwischen den Schichten zur Raumbeheizung dient.

Die Integration wie auch die Addition sind langfristig die wirtschaftlicheren Alternativen: Durch die Materialeinsparung liegen die Investitionskosten niedriger als bei der Applikation, und die Photovoltaik übernimmt zusätzlich zur Stromerzeugung noch Aufgaben der Gebäudehülle.

Generelle Aspekte

Um eine willkürliche Modulanordnung und somit eine Beeinträchtigung der Gesamterscheinung zu vermeiden, muss eine strukturelle Entwurfslogik aus den Gebäudeproportionen heraus entwickelt werden. Bei Fassaden lassen sich verschiedene aus der Architektur des Gebäudes abgeleitete Flächen für die Modulanbringung definieren; dies können zum Beispiel horizontale Bänder unter bzw. über den Fenstern sein, Gesimse oder vertikale, etwa durch Wandpfeiler vorgegebene Zonierungen. Wenn nicht das ganze Dach belegt werden soll, können Photovoltaikmodule auf separaten Flächen wie Gauben oder Vordächern angeordnet werden, ebenso beispielsweise entlang der oberen oder unteren Dachrandbereiche.

Die veranschlagte Nutzungsdauer einer Photovoltaikanlage beträgt ca. 30 Jahre. Dementsprechend müssen Tragkonstruktion und Befestigungselemente aus dauerhaften Materialien wie Aluminium, Edelstahl oder verzinktem Stahl gefertigt werden. Hinterlüftete Konstruktionen für Dach oder Fassade tragen dazu bei, Wasserdampfkondensation und Stauwärme, die sich auf der Rückseite der Module bilden und bei Überhitzung die Energieausbeute mindern, zu vermeiden. Sorgfältige Abdichtung ist erforderlich, um die Korrosion von Verbindungsteilen zu verhindern.

Alle drei Ebenen, die energietechnische, die gestalterische und die konstruktive, müssen bei der Planung gleichberechtigt behandelt werden, um Zusammenspiel, Abhängigkeiten und Schwerpunkte abwägen zu können und ein auf allen Ebenen zufriedenstellendes Ergebnis zu erreichen.

Bereits in einem frühen Planungsstadium sollten Architekt, Fachingenieur und Bauherr sich nach geeigneten Modulfabrikaten und Installationsmöglichkeiten umsehen. Der Photovoltaikmarkt ist vielfältig und in stetiger Veränderung begriffen. Standardisierung führt zu preiswerteren Produkten, Spezialisierung eröffnet der Technologie immer neue gestalterische Ausdrucksformen. Es muss im Einzelfall entschieden werden, welche Produkte der individuellen baulichen Situation und den finanziellen Möglichkeiten des Bauherrn am besten entsprechen.

Vor die Mauer gesetzt und gestalterisch angepasst
in Marbach am Neckar / Deutschland

Design adaptation, attached to wall
in Marbach am Neckar / Germany

Dachhaut aus vorhandenen Ziegeln und neu installierten
photovoltaischen Elementen in Bremen / Deutschland

*Roof cladding made of existing rooftiles and newly
installed photovoltaic elements in Bremen / Germany*

Both the shading of interior spaces as well as the energy efficiency of a combined photovoltaic shading system can be optimised by using a tracking system that follows the daily and seasonal course of the sun. Ventilated photovoltaic façades provide a good multi-functional alternative to the frequently used natural stone façades and can fulfil representative functions just as well.

The integration of photovoltaic modules involves them becoming fully functioning parts of the building shell. The integration of photovoltaics therefore requires a holistic product development, for instance of compound modules that assume all functions of a roof surface (either as small ventilated roof modules or large-scale non-ventilated roof elements). Other solutions include photovoltaic cells integrated into thermopane glazing and providing anti-glare and eyesight protection, or solar double façades which power air-conditioning during the summer and contribute to the heating in winter through the heat accumulated between the layers.

In the long term, addition and integration are the more economically viable solutions. When compared to the attachment method, these application types require lower financial investment, as they are less material-intensive and the photovoltaic panels fulfil dual roles as both power generators and parts of the exterior building structure.

General Aspects

The composition of the solar panels has to be informed by the building proportions in order to avoid an arbitrary allocation of modules, which may have a negative effect on the overall appearance. The modules on the façade may be placed differently according to the architecture of the building: appropriate areas are e.g. horizontal strips below or above windows, cornices or vertical zones structured by pilasters. If the solar panels are not supposed to cover the entire roof area, they can also be positioned on separate areas such as dormers or canopies, or alongside the upper or lower roof edges.

The life-expectancy of a photovoltaic facility is estimated at around thirty years. Accordingly, the corresponding sub-structure and fixings have to be made from durable materials such as aluminium, stainless or galvanised steel. Ventilated roof and façade structures will help prevent condensation or heat accumulation behind modules, which may affect their performance negatively. Careful sealing is required in order to avoid the corrosion of connecting elements.

The same care and attention must be accorded to all three levels of the design process – energy engineering, architectural design and structure – to be able to assess the correlations, interdependencies and emphases of the design and to achieve a result that is equally satisfying on all these levels.

From an early stage in the design process onwards, architects, engineers and building owners should enquire into appropriate photovoltaic products and relevant possibilities of installation. The photovoltaics market is highly versatile and in a state of constant flux. Standardisation leads to lower product costs, while specialisation paves the way towards ever-new architectural expressions of the technology. It must be decided upon individually in each case, which products suit best the specific project and the financial resources of the client.

Innovative Zellen und Module

Innovative Cells and Modules

Die Gestaltung der gängigen, auf dem Markt erhältlichen Photovoltaikmodule – dunkelblaue oder schwarze Farbe, sichtbare metallische Leiterbahnen, glänzende Oberflächen – erschwert ihre Anwendung an Altbauten und Denkmälern oder in der Landschaft. Die Entwicklung einer Modulästhetik, die eine gestalterisch sensible Integration in diese Bereiche ermöglicht, erfordert innovative und kreative Ansätze, muss jedoch auch die Kriterien finanzieller und technischer Machbarkeit berücksichtigen.

Die Zusammenarbeit zwischen Designern und Technologieproduzenten im Rahmen des eurpäischen Forschungs- und Demonstrationsprojektes PVACCEPT war deshalb von Anfang an auf die Entwicklung marktfähiger Produkte ausgerichtet: Es wurden Lösungen gesucht und gefunden, die minimalen technischen Aufwand mit einem Maximum an überzeugender Ästhetik und Übertragbarkeit verbinden. Dabei fand eine Konzentration auf die für eine Vermarktung besonders interessant erscheinenden Entwicklungslinien statt, nämlich Semitransparenz, Oberflächenstruktur, Farbe und multifunktionale Einzelobjekte.

The design of available standard modules – dark blue or black in colour, visible metal conductors, shiny surfaces – complicates their employment on old buildings or monuments and in landscapes. Innovative and creative approaches are necessary to develop an aesthetic design, which enables an architecturally sensitive application of photovoltaic modules in these fields. At the same time the criteria of financial and technical feasibility have to be considered.

The cooperation of designers and technology producers within the European research and demonstration project PVACCEPT aimed therefore at the development of marketable products from the very beginning. Solutions were sought and found, which combine a minimum of technical intervention with a maximum of convincing aesthetics and transferability. They concentrated on those development lines which appear as especially interesting for the market, namely semitransparency, surface structure, colour and multi-functional objects.

Als Ausgangsbasis für den Entwicklungsprozess wurden Dünnschichtmodule gegenüber kristallinen Siliziummodulen bevorzugt, da sie bereits ein deutlich homogeneres Erscheinungsbild haben, das mehr Gestaltungsmöglichkeiten eröffnet. Aber auch monokristalline Solarzellen, die in unterschiedliche Materialien und Formen eingebettet werden können, haben das Potential für neue und variable Entwicklungen. Die unterschiedlichen Herstellungsprozesse führten zu verschiedenen Schwerpunkten in Bezug auf die innovativen Entwicklungen (vgl. Kapitel „Technische Grundlagen"). Insbesondere die Unterschiede in der Produktion von Kupfer-Indium-Diselenid- (CIS-) und Kadmium-Tellurid- (CdTe-) Modulen sollen hier kurz dargestellt werden. Bei den CdTe-Modulen ist das Deckglas, das später dem Licht zugewandt ist, das Substrat – das heißt der Träger – für die Beschichtung mit Zellen. Bei den CIS-Modulen ist es das Rückglas, das dem Licht zugewandt ist. Auf dieses wird nach dem Schicht- und Zellherstellungsprozess ein zweites Glas auflaminiert. Während dieses Herstellungsprozesses, den die Substratgläser komplett durchlaufen müssen, werden sie auf Temperaturen von 400–500°C erhitzt. In jedem Fall kann eine Modifizierung des Erscheinungsbildes der Module nur durch Modifizierung des dem Licht zugewandten Glases erfolgen. Im Falle des CdTe-Moduls muss dieses Glas, da es Substrat ist, einen thermischen Prozess bei 500°C durchlaufen; bei dem CIS-Modul, bei dem das dem Licht zugewandte Glas später auflaminiert wird, ist die thermische Belastung geringer (ca. 200°C). Es ist zwar prinzipiell möglich, bei CdTe-Modulen strukturiertes oder farbig gestaltetes Glas als Substrat zu verwenden, dies bringt aber in der Praxis technische Probleme und Risiken mit sich und kann zu Ausfällen im Produktionsprozess führen. Weitere Tests und Experimente wären nötig, um diesbezüglich zu endgültigen Lösungen zu kommen. Hierfür fehlten im Rahmen des Projektes sowohl die finanziellen Mittel als auch die Zeit. Natürlich kann bei CdTe-Modulen nach Fertigstellung auf das dem Licht zugewandte Glas ein weiteres Deckglas mit speziellen Eigenschaften laminiert werden. Dies führt allerdings zu einem deutlich erhöhten Gesamtgewicht des Moduls. Wenn zum Beispiel ein 2 mm dickes Glas hierfür verwendet wird, erhöht sich das Modulgewicht von 16 kg auf 20 kg.

Die gestalterischen Modifikationen beschränkten sich entsprechend auf die thermisch bei der Produktion weniger belasteten Deckgläser der CIS-Module, während bei den neuen Entwicklungen an CdTe-Modulen der Schwerpunkt auf anderen Aspekten lag, beispielsweise der Entwicklung von Modulen, die auf der Baustelle unterschiedlichen Maßen angepasst werden können (*cut-to-size*).

Das Herstellen von semitransparenten Modulen war in beiden Fällen möglich.

Die monokristallinen Zellen wurden ebenfalls mit spezifischen Methoden bearbeitet, um sie semitransparent zu gestalten. Sie wurden vor allem verwendet, um multifunktionale Einzelobjekte – wie sogenannte „Solarflaggen" oder selbsttragende Pergola-Elemente – damit zu bestücken. Es zeigte sich, dass es schon mit vergleichsweise einfachen Mitteln möglich ist, Photovoltaikmodule aus Dünnschichtzellen oder mit eingebetteten monokristallinen Zellen den besonderen gestalterischen Erfordernissen von Altbauumgebungen und Landschaften anzupassen. Die Einsatzmöglichkeiten der Photovoltaik werden damit erheblich erweitert.

Auch die Analyse der Energiekreisläufe und Umwelteinflüsse der von PVACCEPT entwickelten innovativen Module (Lebenszyklusanalyse) ergab eine positive Bewertung; insbesondere Dünnschichtsysteme können unter diesen Gesichtspunkten, obwohl noch in einem frühen Entwicklungsstadium befindlich, bereits jetzt als zufriedenstellend betrachtet werden.

Einige der innovativen Prototypen fanden Anwendung in den PVACCEPT-Demonstrationsanlagen in Italien und Deutschland, die seit Mitte des Jahres 2004 in Betrieb sind. Die Energieerträge aller Anlagen entsprachen bisher den Kalkulationen.

Die hier dargestellten technologischen Grundlagen geben den Stand der Technik zu Beginn des Projektes (2001) wieder; die PVACCEPT-Projektergebnisse stammen aus den Jahren 2002 bis 2004. In der Zwischenzeit haben selbstverständlich weitere innovative Entwicklungen stattgefunden. Wann immer die Planung einer Photovoltaikinstallation in Angriff genommen wird, sollten sich die Projektbeteiligten deshalb über den aktuellen Stand der Technik informieren.

Thin-film modules were preferred to crystalline silicon modules as basis for the development process, as their appearance is clearly more homogeneous, opening more possibilities for design variations. Furthermore, monocrystalline solar cells, which can be integrated into different materials and shapes, have the potential for new and variable development. The distinct production processes led to differing emphases with regard to the innovative developments. (Please see chapter "Technical Basics".)

In this context the differences between the production processes of copper-indium-diselenide (CIS) and cadmium-telluride (CdTe) modules are of importance: For CdTe-modules the front glass, which is later exposed to the sun, is the substrate – i.e. the carrier – onto which the films representing the cells are deposited and onto which the second (protective) glass is laminated later on. For CIS-modules the substrate glass, onto which the films are deposited, is later on turned away from the sun and the second glass, which is laminated onto this first glass is turned towards the sun. During the production processes, to which the substrates have to be subjected, maximum temperatures of 400 to 500°C have to be achieved for good-quality materials. In any case, a modification of the visual appearance of the module must be achieved on the glass turned towards the sun. In the case of CdTe this glass, being the substrate glass, has to undergo the thermal heating of up to 500°C. In the case of the CIS-module, the glass, which is turned towards the sun and is laminated onto the substrate later on, experiences a lower thermal strain at 200°C. It is basically possible to use structured or coloured glass for CdTe as substrate, but this brings about technical problems and risks, which may lead to glass breakage and stop the whole production process. Only after undertaking additional tests and experiments could such an option be applied. During the project there was neither sufficient time nor funding for such experimentation. Evidently, after finishing a CdTe-module, a printed or coloured glass sheet can be laminated onto the substrate glass, which this time only experiences a temperature of around 200°C. This will, however, lead to an increased module weight. If, for example, a 2 mm thick glass is used for this purpose, the total module weight will be 20 kg instead of 16 kg.

Correspondingly, the design modifications were restricted to the front glass panes of CIS-modules, which are put under less thermal strain during the production process, while the new developments on the basis of CdTe-modules focussed on other aspects, for example the development of modules, which can be adapted in size on the building site ("cut-to-size").

The production of semitransparent modules was possible for both technologies.

Monocrystalline cells were also treated with specific techniques to reach semitransparent design. They were used, above all, to equip single multi-functional objects such as "solar flags" or self-supporting pergola elements. It has proved that photovoltaic thin-film modules or modules with embedded monocrystalline cells can be adapted to the special architectural requirements of an existing building or landscape context with relatively simple means. This opens up a whole new range of possibilities for photovoltaic application.

Furthermore, the analysis of the innovative PVACCEPT modules with regard to energy cycles and environmental impact (life cycle analysis) resulted in a positive assessment. Thin-film modules in particular, although they are still in an early stage of development, can already be regarded as satisfactory in this respect.

Some of the innovative prototypes were implemented in the PVACCEPT demonstration facilities in Italy and Germany, which have been functioning since the middle of the year 2004. Up to now, the energy yield of all facilities has met the expectations.

The state of the art of the technological basics as presented here is 2001; the project results originate from 2002 to 2004. In the meantime, of course, other innovative developments have taken place in parallel, both on the technical and design level. Therefore it is recommendable that, before starting the (architectural) planning of a photovoltaic facility, all those involved should get informed and be on top of the latest technological developments.

Semitransparente PVACCEPT-Testmodule und -Prototypen
(Dünnschichttechnologie)
Semitransparent PVACCEPT test modules and prototypes
(thin-film technology)

Semitransparenz

Semitransparenz von Photovoltaikzellen und -modulen ist ein wichtiger Gestaltungsaspekt, der neue Anwendungsmöglichkeiten erschließt und gute Möglichkeiten für die Architekturintegration bietet. Werden semitransparente Module – unter Verwendung von Isolierglas oder einer zusätzlichen Glasscheibe – in Fassaden oder Dächer als Teile der Gebäudehülle eingebaut, wird dadurch in den darunter oder dahinter liegenden Räumen ein reizvolles Muster und Spiel aus Licht und Schatten erzeugt. Semitransparente Solarzellen, in Glas oder Kunststoff eingebettet, eignen sich darüber hinaus gut für die Gestaltung multifunktionaler Einzelobjekte, die Stromerzeugung, Beleuchtung und weitere Funktionen kombinieren (zum Beispiel Straßenmöblierung), aber auch für den Ersatz von Wintergartenverglasungen. Die semitransparente Wirkung kann auf verschiedene Weise hervorgerufen werden: zum einen durch die Einbettung von Zellen mit größeren Abständen dazwischen, zum anderen durch mechanische Eingriffe direkt in die Zellen, also etwa durch Laser-Verdampfung von Teilflächen, durch Ritzen oder Fräsen. Auf diese Weise kann Semitransparenz in unterschiedlichster Form, zum Beispiel als Streifen- oder Rundlochmuster, erzeugt werden. Die Breite der Streifen ist variabel und kann den spezifischen architektonischen Erfordernissen angepasst werden.

Die erzeugten Muster können mit Bedruckung oder farbigen Rückgläsern kombiniert werden, was die Anwendungsmöglichkeiten noch erweitert. Zahlreiche Varianten sind möglich: Vorstellbar wäre beispielsweise ein semitransparentes Modul mit Streifen, welches die Maßstäblichkeit von Ziegeln und Fugen einer Mauer sowie deren Farbigkeit aufnimmt und an einer Tür oder anderen Fassadenelementen eingesetzt wird, mit denen es so zu einer gestalterischen Einheit verschmilzt.

Die geschilderten Variationen an Zellen und Modulen machen die Photovoltaikinstallation zu einem aktiven architektonischen Gestaltungselement mit erweiterten Einsatzmöglichkeiten. Zu berücksichtigen ist dabei, dass alle Maßnahmen zur Erzeugung von Semitransparenz an Zellen und Modulen dazu führen, dass ein entsprechender Anteil an Oberfläche für die Stromerzeugung nicht mehr genutzt werden kann. Dies muss von vornherein bei der Ertrags- und Flächenkalkulation berücksichtigt werden.

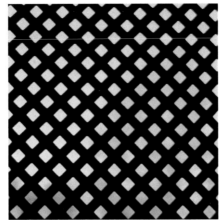

Semitransparente PVACCEPT-Testmodule
(Dünnschichttechnologie)
Semitransparent PVACCEPT test modules
(thin-film technology)

Semitransparency

Semitransparency of photovoltaic cells and modules is an important design feature, offering new application possibilities and providing good potential for architectural integration. When integrating semitransparent modules into roofs or façades as part of the building shell – using thermopane glazing or an additional sheet of glass – an attractive interplay of light and shadow in the spaces below and beyond is created. Furthermore, plastic or glass embedded semitransparent solar cells are well suited for the design of multifunctional objects, which combine power generation, lighting and other functions (for instance so-called street furniture), but also as a replacement of conservatory glazing. There are various ways of creating this semitransparent effect: Firstly, by spacing the embedded cells at larger distances from each other; secondly, by mechanical modification of the cells, i.e. laser-evaporation of parts of the surface, scratching or milling. In this way, a broad spectrum of semitransparent patterns can be created, for example stripes or punch-hole patterns. The transparency factor of the surfaces, for example the width of the stripes, can be varied to suit specific architectural requirements.

The transparency patterns can be combined with screen-printing or tinted back glasses, thus further expanding the range of possible applications. Numerous variations can be created, for example semitransparent modules with stripes, which take up the dimensional grid of bricks and joints in a wall, as well as their colours, and could be applied to doors or other parts of the façade, thus merging the different architectural elements.

The aforementioned range of cell and module variations makes photovoltaics an active element of architectural design with an extended applicability. It has to be considered, however, that all measures taken to create semitransparency automatically reduce the active surface of cells and modules available for power generation. This has to be taken into account beforehand when calculating energy yield and required surface area.

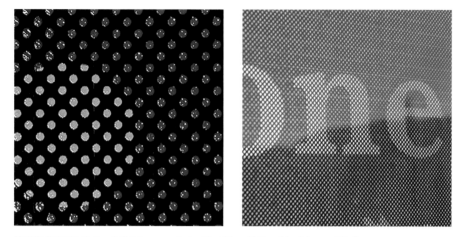

PVACCEPT-Testmodule und -Prototypen von bedruckten Dünnschichtmodulen (Idee geschützt)
PVACCEPT test modules and prototypes of screen-printed thin-film modules (idea protected)

Farbe und Muster

Aus physikalischen Gründen (vgl. Kapitel „Technische Grundlagen") ist die Farbpalette von Solarzellen eingeschränkt. Kristalline und amorphe Siliziumzellen sind üblicherweise blau. Andere Farbtöne können durch Modifikation der Antireflexschicht erzeugt werden, führen aber zu einem etwas geringerem Wirkungsgrad. Dünnschichtsolarzellen aus amorphem Silizium oder CIS sind schwarz, CdTe-Zellen schimmern grünlich.

Diese Standard-Modulfarben stehen vielfach in zu starkem Kontrast zu den gedeckten Farbtönen gealterter Baustoffe oder den natürlichen Umgebungsfarben bei einer Installation in der Landschaft. Mit der von PVACCEPT entwickelten Methode kann die Farbe von Dünnschichtmodulen verändert werden, ohne in deren Technologie oder Produktionsprozess einzugreifen. Es sind allerdings zusätzliche Arbeitsschritte notwendig, die von den Modulherstellern an Subunternehmer ausgelagert werden müssen und zusätzliche Kosten erzeugen.

Der Vorteil der Methode liegt darin, dass jedes beliebige Muster und jede gewünschte Farbigkeit mit ein und derselben Technik (keramischer Siebdruck) erzeugt werden kann. PVACCEPT verwendete Vierfarbdruck oder Druck mit Schmuckfarben in Abhängigkeit von der Komplexität des Motivs. Das gewünschte Muster wird in einem gleichmäßigen Punktraster auf das Deckglas des Moduls gedruckt. Die Regelmäßigkeit des Rasters ist wichtig, um das einwandfreie Funktionieren des Moduls trotz der Abdeckung eines Teils seiner Oberfläche zu gewährleisten. Der Anteil an bedruckter Fläche sollte so gering wie möglich gehalten werden, da der Ertrag des Moduls durch einen entsprechenden Prozentsatz reduziert wird. Die Prototypen wurden mit einem Bedruckungsgrad von 10 und 20 Prozent hergestellt. Auch Texte oder Logos können auf diese Weise erzeugt werden, so dass Photovoltaikmodule bisher nicht mögliche zusätzliche Aufgaben (Information, Werbung) übernehmen können.

Bei der Gestaltung der Farbigkeit muss berücksichtigt werden, dass der größte Teil der Moduloberfläche weiterhin die Originalfarbe Schwarz (oder Dunkelgrün) aufweist, was die generelle Farberscheinung beeinflusst. Der endgültige Farbeindruck entsteht sozusagen im Auge des Betrachters unter Berücksichtigung des dunklen Hintergrundes, was bedeutet, dass wesentlich leuchtendere und hellere Farben für den Druck verwendet werden müssen, als in der farblichen Gesamterscheinung vorgesehen. Es können daher mehrere Testdrucke notwendig sein, bis der gewünschte Farbeindruck erreicht ist.

PVACCEPT-Testmodule und -Prototypen von bedruckten Dünnschichtmodulen (Idee geschützt)
PVACCEPT test modules and prototypes of screen-printed thin-film modules (idea protected)

Physical reasons (refer to chapter "Technical Basics") limit the colour range of solar cells. Crystalline and amorphous silicon cells are usually blue. By modifying the antireflection layer it is possible to create other colours, which leads, however, to a slightly lower cell efficiency. Thin-film solar cells consisting of amorphous silicon or CIS are black in colour; CdTe-cells have a greenish shimmer.

These standard colours are mostly in stark contrast to the subtle shades of aged building materials or the natural colours of the environment if the facility is located in landscapes. By applying the method developed by PVACCEPT, the colour of thin-film modules can be altered without changing their technology or the production process. However, this method requires additional production steps that usually have to be outsourced to subcontractors and generate extra costs.

The advantage of this method lies in the possibility of producing any kind of pattern or colour by using the same technique (ceramic screen-printing). PVACCEPT used four-colour printing or printing with ornamental colours depending on the complexity of the motif. The required pattern is printed onto the cover glass of the module in a regular dot grid. A regular grid is necessary to sustain full functionality of the modules despite the fact that part of their surface is covered up. The percentage of printed surface area should be reduced to a minimum, as the energy yield of the module will be reduced by an analogous percentage. The prototypes were produced with a 10 and 20 percent degree of printed surface. Even lettering or logos can be created with this technique, enabling photovoltaic modules to take over completely new additional functions (information, advertisement).

When designing the colour appearance it has to be considered that the main part of the module surface will remain in its original black (or dark green) colour. This affects the overall colour appearance. In other words: The final optical colour impression is created in the viewer's eye in relation to the dark background. To compensate for this effect, much brighter and more brilliant colours have to be used for printing than planned for the overall colour scheme. Several test prints may therefore be necessary to reach the desired colour impression.

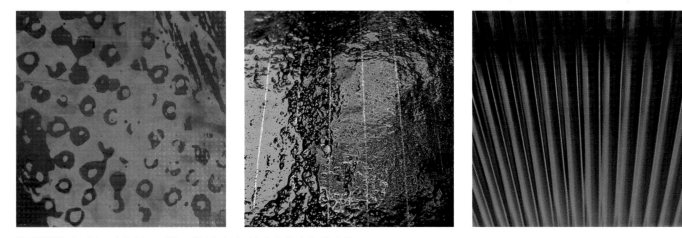

PVACCEPT-Testmodule und -Prototypen (Dünnschichttechnologie) mit strukturierten Deckgläsern

PVACCEPT test modules and prototypes (thin-film technology) with structured front glass panes

Oberflächenstruktur

Glas, wie es überwiegend als Modulvorderseite verwendet wird, kontrastiert durch seine glatte, gleichmäßige, glänzende Oberfläche stark mit den matten und oft unebenen bzw. unregelmäßigen Oberflächen von traditionellen Baumaterialien wie Mauerwerk, Putz oder Dachziegeln. Die Lichtreflexion auf den Glasflächen macht die Module weithin sichtbar und führt manchmal auch zu einem unerwünschten Blendungseffekt.

Um eine bessere Anpassung an vorhandene Materialien und Strukturen sowie eine größere Unauffälligkeit zu erzielen, wurden von PVACCEPT Experimente mit verschiedenen Arten von Deckgläsern durchgeführt. Mit einfachen Mitteln und vor allem ohne Ertragsverluste wurden dabei ästhetisch ansprechende Ergebnisse erzielt.

Sandstrahlen des Glases erwies sich als geeignete Methode, um matte Oberflächen zu erzielen; außerdem können mit dieser Methode alle möglichen regelmäßigen oder unregelmäßigen Muster umgesetzt werden. Die sandgestrahlten Teile erscheinen in einem hellen Grau, was die Kombination der Module sogar mit sehr hellen Fassadenflächen ermöglicht.

Ein anderer Ansatz bestand darin, Strukturglas verschiedener Typen als Deckglas zu verwenden, um eine mattierende Wirkung zu erzielen. Im Rahmen der von PVACCEPT durchgeführten Tests wurde ein besonderer Effekt durch ein Profilglas mit kleinteiliger Pyramidenstruktur auf einem Kadmium-Tellurid-Dünnschichtmodul erzeugt: Die dunkelgrüne Modulfarbe wurde dadurch betont und erschien als leuchtendes Grün, dessen Tönung unter verschiedenen Lichteinfallswinkeln changiert. Dieses Modul ist somit hervorragend geeignet für Anwendungen in der Landschaft.

Der besondere Vorteil der Verwendung strukturierter Deckgläser liegt darin, dass auf dem Markt erhältliche preiswerte Standardgläser benutzt werden können und keine besonderen Eingriffe in den Modulherstellungsprozess erforderlich sind. Man sollte lediglich bedenken, dass strukturierte Gläser möglicherweise etwas leichter verschmutzen als glatte Gläser und deshalb ab und zu gereinigt werden müssen, da Verschmutzung die Funktion der Module beeinträchtigt.

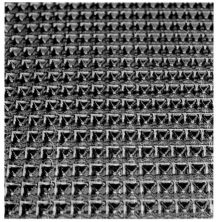

PVACCEPT-Testmodule und -Prototypen (Dünnschichttechnologie) mit strukturierten Deckgläsern
PVACCEPT test modules and prototypes (thin-film technology) with structured front glass panes

Surface Structure

Glass as an even, regular and shiny material that is commonly used as module cover, strongly contrasts with the matt and uneven respectively irregular finish of traditional building materials like brick, render or roof tiles. Reflections on its surface make the modules highly visible at a distance and occasionally cause undesirable glare. PVACCEPT addressed the issue of better and more inconspicuous adaptation to existing materials and structures in a number of experiments with various types of cover glass. Aesthetically convincing results were achieved with simple means and, above all, without compromising the performance of the modules.

Sandblasting proved to be a suitable procedure to create matted surfaces; as a further advantage, this method enables the production of all kinds of regular and irregular patterns. The sandblasted parts appear in a light grey, thus even allowing their combination with very bright façades.

Another approach consisted of the use of various types of structured glass as cover glass to create a matt finish. Within the tests carried out by PVACCEPT a special effect was achieved by applying figured glass with a pyramidal surface structure on top of a cadmium-telluride thin-film module: The dark green colour of the module was intensified by the light refraction and appeared as brilliant green, the shades of which changed under different angles of incident light. Thus this module is highly suitable for use in natural landscapes.

The particular advantage of the application of figured cover glass lies in the fact that this is an easily available and cheap "off-the-shelf" product and does not hamper the normal production process of the modules. One should just bear in mind that figured glass may possibly collect dirt more easily than smooth glass and might have to be cleaned from time to time to avoid negative effects on the performance of the modules.

„Solar Flag"-Testmodul mit monokristallinen Zellen und
integrierter Beleuchtung
*"Solar flag" test module with monocrystalline cells and
integrated illumination*

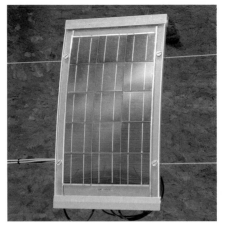
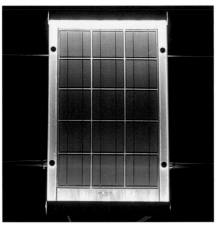

Multifunktionale Objekte

Multifunktionale Photovoltaiknutzungen findet
man bereits häufiger im öffentlichen Raum,
etwa in Form von Straßenmöbeln oder künstlerischen Objekten. PVACCEPT entwickelte
Elemente, sogenannte *solar flags* („Solarflaggen"), die in verschiedenen Größen hergestellt und in beliebiger Zahl aneinandergereiht
werden können. Die *solar flags* bestehen aus
semitransparenten grauen Solarzellen, einer
Sonderentwicklung, die zwischen leicht gekrümmte Acrylglasscheiben eingebettet wurden. Die Elemente sind selbstleuchtend und
geben die während des Tages erzeugte und
gespeicherte Energie nachts an integrierte
LED (*light emitting diodes* = Leuchtdioden)
ab. Ihre Farbe, das heißt sowohl die Farbe des
Moduls selbst wie auch die Farbe der Leuchtdioden, ist variabel. Zusätzlich kann moderne
RGB-Technik (Rot-Grün-Blau) zur Steuerung
von Farbverläufen der Beleuchtung problemlos
einbezogen werden. Die Bandbreite der Einsatzmöglichkeiten reicht vom „Solarbaum" bis
zur dauerhaften oder temporären Installation
über Plätzen und Straßen, um eine besondere Atmosphäre für kulturelle Veranstaltungen
zu schaffen. Zusätzlich können die *solar flags*
eine Funktion als Werbeträger übernehmen,
wo dies angemessen ist.

Solare Pergola-Elemente sind ebenfalls vielsei-
tig einsetzbar und können ganz unterschiedlich gestaltet werden. Als Prototypen wurden
sowohl semitransparente Glas/Glas-Module
in Dünnschichttechnologie und Sondergrößen
wie auch selbsttragende Acrylglaselemente
mit eingebetteten Solarzellen hergestellt. Auch
diese Elemente können mit integrierter Beleuchtung kombiniert werden.

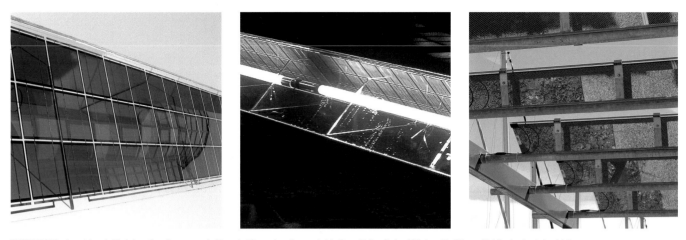

PVACCEPT-Testmodul und -Prototyp: Semitransparente Pergola-Elemente mit monokristallinen Zellen (links, Mitte) und in Dünnschichttechnologie (rechts)
PVACCEPT test module and prototype: Semitransparent pergola elements with monocrystalline cells (left, middle) and in thin-film technology (right)

Multifunctional photovoltaic applications are already to be encountered quite frequently in public space, for example in the form of street furniture or artistic objects. PVACCEPT developed so-called "solar flags", which can be produced in various sizes and added in any number. The "solar flags" consist of special semi-transparent, grey solar cells, which are embedded between slightly bent acrylic glass panes. The elements are luminous and at night they give off the energy generated and stored during the day by powering integrated light emitting diodes (LEDs). Their colour can be varied, which goes both for the colour of the module itself and the colour of the LEDs. Additionally, modern RGB-technology (red, green, blue) can be incorporated without problems to control colour gradients of the lighting. The range of applications reaches from so-called "solar trees" to temporary or permanent installations in public space creating a special atmosphere for cultural events. Additionally, the "solar flags" can, where appropriate, take over the function of an advertising medium.

Solar pergola elements also permit a flexible range of uses and designs. Respective prototypes were produced as semitransparent glass/glass thin-film modules in special sizes and as self-supporting acrylic elements with embedded solar cells. These elements may incorporate light fittings as well.

Multifunctional Objects

PVACCEPT-Testmodul mit umlaufendem Glasrand
(Dünnschichttechnologie)
PVACCEPT test module with glass rim (thin-film technology)

Cut-to-Size-Module

Die *cut-to-size*-Modulprototypen entsprachen dem Wunsch, Module zu entwickeln, die direkt auf der Baustelle maßlich noch angepasst werden können. Dies sollte der Tatsache Rechnung tragen, dass bei Altbauten häufig erhebliche Maßtoleranzen bei allen Bauteilen festzustellen sind.

Hierfür wurde das Substratglas nach seiner Beschichtung mit Zellen nicht wie üblich auf eine Glasplatte gleicher Größe, sondern auf eine größere Glasplatte laminiert, so dass ein umlaufender Rand aus einfachem Glas verblieb. Dieser Glasrand kann dann von Hand mit dem Glasschneider passend zurechtgeschnitten werden, ohne dass das eigentliche Modul, das selbst nicht geschnitten werden darf, beschädigt wird.

Ein ähnliches Verfahren wurde angewendet, um sogenannte Modul-Lamellen herzustellen. In diesem Fall wurden 60 cm x 120 cm große Glasplatten mit 30 cm x 120 cm großen, mit Zellen beschichteten Glasplatten zusammengefügt, so dass die eine Hälfte der Glasplatte transparent blieb. Eine gestaffelte Anbringung solcher Module als Sonnenschutz ergibt interessante gestalterische Effekte.

Da sich die Herstellung von Prototypen mit fortschreitendem Projektverlauf zunehmend auf die Produktion für die geplanten Demonstrationsstandorte konzentrieren musste und für die *cut-to-size*-Module kein konkreter Anwendungsfall vorlag, blieben diese Neuentwicklungen im Teststadium. Noch zu lösende Probleme liegen in der Anwendungstechnik; beispielsweise müssen beim Einsatz als Überkopfverglasung (Sicherheitsglas) Genehmigungen der Baubehörden eingeholt werden. Diese werden in der Regel für mit EVA-Folie laminierte Module problemlos erteilt.

PVACCEPT-Testmodule in Lamellenstruktur
(Dünnschichttechnologie)
PVACCEPT test modules as lamellae (thin-film techno-
logy)

Cut-to-Size Modules

The development of cut-to-size module prototypes had the aim of providing modules whose size can be adapted directly on site to the often-encountered substantial tolerances in the dimensions of old buildings.

To achieve this, the substrate glass was, after its coating with cells, laminated onto a larger pane of glass and not, as is usually the case, onto a pane of the same size, thus leaving a rim of ordinary glass around the module on all sides. This rim can then be cut-to-size by hand without damaging the actual module, which cannot be cut.

In a similar way so-called module lamellae were produced: 30 cm x 120 cm panes coated with cells were laminated onto 60 cm x 120 cm glass panes, leaving half of the pane transparent. Arranging these modules like solar protection louvers results in interesting architectural effects.

In the course of the project the prototypes were increasingly produced for application in the selected demonstration objects and, as no real-life project put itself forward for implementation of the cut–to-size modules, these new developments did not make it beyond the testing stage. The issues yet to be resolved are related to the field of applications engineering; the employment of the modules as part of overhead glazing (safety glass), for instance, requires planning permission. This permission is usually granted without problems for modules which are laminated with EVA-foil.

Gelungene Praxisbeispiele

Best Practice Examples

Im Folgenden werden exemplarisch einige gelungene Beispiele für die Anwendung von Photovoltaik auf Dächern und an Fassaden im Altbau, im städtischen Raum und in der Landschaft vorgestellt. Sie illustrieren die Vielfalt der Gestaltungsvarianten, die mit innovativen Modulen, aber auch schon mit Standardmodulen möglich sind.

Die Darstellung in Form von Photos und Kurzbeschreibungen basiert auf Informationen, die von Bauherren oder Architekten zur Verfügung gestellt wurden. Sie verzichtet bewusst sowohl auf detaillierte konstruktive Maßnahmenbeschreibungen wie auch auf die Erläuterung durch technische Zeichnungen. Der Grund liegt darin, dass gerade Projekte im Altbaubereich sehr individuell sind und viele technische Details speziell für das jeweilige Vorhaben entwickelt werden müssen, so dass eine Übertragbarkeit der technischen Aspekte nur bedingt gegeben ist. Aus demselben Grund wurde auf Kostenangaben verzichtet. Auch werden die Projekte nicht in der Gesamtheit der baulichen Maßnahmen wiedergegeben, sondern im Mittelpunkt steht stets die kreativ gestaltete oder gut integrierte Photovoltaikanlage.

Auf der Grundlage der Angaben zu den Standorten, Bauherren, Architekten, Fachingenieuren und Systemhersteller hat jeder weitergehend Interessierte die Möglichkeit, sich umfassender über die einzelnen Projekte zu informieren.

In the following chapter a number of best practice examples of photovoltaic applications on roofs and façades of old buildings, in urban space and in the context of landscapes are presented. They are intended to illustrate the manifold design variations that can be realised with innovative as well as standard photovoltaic modules.

The photos and short descriptions included are based on information made available by the building owners or the architects. Detailed technical descriptions and drawings are deliberately not included. The reason is that projects dealing with existing buildings or an existing urban or landscape context are highly distinct. Their design parameters are very individual and technical details have to be developed specifically for the relevant context, thus being only of limited transferability. The same applies to cost details, which have not been included for the same reason. Moreover, the project descriptions do not include the complete construction measures but focus always on the creatively designed or well integrated photovoltaic system.

Details about the locations, owners, architects, special engineers and photovoltaic producers provide a basis for further information to anyone who is interested in finding out more about the projects.

Anmerkung

Die wichtigsten Daten zu den einzelnen Projekten können aus Platzgründen nur in Englisch dargestellt werden. Die englischen Begriffe werden deshalb hier einmal in der deutschen Bedeutung wiedergegeben:

Location:	Standort
Owner:	Bauherr
Architect:	Architekt
Energy consultant:	Energieberater
System provider:	Systemhersteller
Year:	Baujahr
Energy output:	Nennleistung
Energy yield:	Jahresertrag
Area:	Fläche

Kirchendächer *Carlow; Bärwalde / Deutschland*

Im Rahmen der Förderinitiative „Kirchengemeinden für die Sonnenenergie" der Deutschen Bundesstiftung Umwelt (DBU) wurden zwischen 1999 und 2001 insgesamt 714 Solaranlagen errichtet, 622 davon als Photovoltaikanlagen. Zu diesen gehören auch die hier gezeigten Installationen auf Kirchendächern, die im Zuge ohnehin fälliger Maßnahmen zur Dachsanierung erfolgten.

Für die Kirche in Carlow wurde ein integratives System gewählt, dessen Hersteller Tondachziegel und polykristalline Module farblich aufeinander abgestimmt anbietet. Die Module wurden in Deckbreite und Länge an die vorhandene Dachdeckung aus Schiefer angepasst; ein Photovoltaikmodul ersetzt dabei sechs Tondachziegel. So blieb das historische Bild der Kirche, den Auflagen der Denkmalpflegebehörde entsprechend, erhalten.

Im Zentrum von Bärwalde steht die 1867 erbaute Dorfkirche, eine einschiffige Hallenkirche. Auf dem verschattungsfreien Süddach wurden in Abstimmung mit der Denkmalpflegebehörde Photovoltaikmodule traufseitig zwischen den zwei gotischen Spitztürmen installiert. Verwendet wurden polykristalline Glas/Folie-Module in denkmalgerechter Anpassung bezüglich Farbe und Größe (1 m x 2 m).

Location:	Carlow, Germany
Owner:	Ev.-luth. Kirchengemeinde
Architect:	Brüning + Evers
Energy consultant:	Dachziegelwerke Pfleiderer
System provider:	Dachziegelwerke Pfleiderer
Year:	2001
Energy output:	5 kW$_p$
Energy yield:	3 700 kWh/a
Area:	50 m^2

Church Roofs

Carlow; Bärwalde / Germany

A total of 714 solar facilities were installed between 1999 and 2001 as part of the funding initiative "Congregations for Solar Energy" run by the environmental foundation *Deutsche Bundesstiftung Umwelt* (DBU). 622 of these are photovoltaic installations. Some examples are shown here. The churches were equipped with photovoltaics in the course of roof repairs that had become necessary.

An integrative system was selected for the church in Carlow. The system manufacturer produces roof tiles and polycrystalline modules in matching colours. The covering width and length of the modules were adapted to the existing slate roofing material; one photovoltaic module replaces six roof tiles. Thus the historical appearance of the church was maintained, as stipulated by the monument protection authority.

The church at Bärwalde, a hall church with a single nave built in 1867, is located in the village centre. Photovoltaic modules were installed on the unshaded south-facing roof on the side of the eaves, between the two Gothic steeples, in agreement with the monument protection authority. Polycrystalline glass/foil modules were used, their colour and size adapted to the listed building (1 m x 2 m).

Location:	Bärwalde, Germany
Owner:	Ev.-luth. Kirchengemeinde
Architect:	Bezirkskirchenamt Dresden
Energy consultant:	Ingenieurbüro Dr. Scheffler & Partner GmbH
System provider:	SachsenSolar AG
Year:	2004
Energy output:	2.1 kW$_p$
Energy yield:	1 780 kWh/a
Area:	40 m^2

Kirchendächer

Plauen; Dresden-Löbtau / Deutschland

Bei beiden hier gezeigten Kirchendächern wurden die gleichen Photovoltaikmodule verwendet, die sich den Naturschieferdächern besonders gut anpassen. Es handelt sich um rahmenlose Module mit monokristallinen schwarzen Zellen. Die besondere Anpassung besteht darin, dass die sichtbaren Metallkontakte (Stromabnehmer) geschwärzt wurden und die rückseitige Folie ebenfalls schwarz statt, wie üblich, weiß oder durchsichtig ist. Die matte Wirkung wird mit einem fein strukturierten hochtransparenten Deckglas erzielt.

In Plauen konnten die farblich dezenten, schieferähnlichen, matt wirkenden Module die Denkmalbehörde nach langen Verhandlungen überzeugen.

Die 1924 errichtete Hallenkirche in Dresden-Löbtau steht ebenfalls unter Denkmalschutz und wurde im Jahr 2004 komplett saniert. In das 60 Grad geneigte und nach Süden ausgerichtete Satteldach aus Naturschiefer wurde dabei eine kleine Photovoltaikanlage integriert. Sie besteht aus einem netzgekoppelten System mit insgesamt 30 Modulen, die in drei Reihen à 10 Modulen angeordnet sind.

Gleichzeitig wurde die Kirche durch einen nach ökologischen Kriterien geplanten Neubau des Gemeindezentrums (mit passiver Solarenergienutzung und auf dem Flachdach aufgeständerter Photovoltaikanlage mit 2,73 kW_p Leistung) ergänzt.

Ursprünglich sollte die gesamte Süd-Dachfläche des Kirchengebäudes mit einer Photovoltaikanlage belegt werden, was an der Ablehnung durch die zuständigen Denkmalschutzbehörden scheiterte. Die Installation der zwei kleineren und örtlich getrennten Anlagen stellt die Kompromisslösung dar, die nach langen Verhandlungen gefunden wurde.

Location:	Plauen, Germany
Owner:	Katholische Pfarrei Herz Jesu
Architect:	Architekturbüro Schaufel
Energy consultant:	SachsenSolar AG
System provider:	Solarwatt
Year:	2001
Energy output:	24 kW_p
Energy yield:	21 500 kWh/a
Area:	192 m²

Church Roofs

Plauen; Dresden-Löbtau / Germany

On both church roofs shown here, the same photovoltaic modules, which are specially suited for roofs covered with natural slate, have been applied. The modules are frameless and contain monocrystalline black solar cells. The special adaptation is reached by dyeing the visible metal contacts (current collectors) black and using a black backing foil rather than the usual white or transparent type. The matt appearance is achieved by using a finely structured highly transparent cover glass.

In Plauen, the subtly coloured, slate-like matt modules were deemed, in long discussions, a convincing solution by the monument protection authority.

The church in Dresden-Löbtau was built in 1924 and is a listed monument, too. It was completely renovated in 2004. A small photovoltaic installation was integrated into the 60° inclined south-oriented gable roof. It consists of a grid-connected system with 30 modules, arranged in three rows of 10 modules each.

At the same time a new community centre was built next to the church and designed following ecological principles. These include the passive use of solar energy and a 2.73 kW$_p$ photovoltaic system, which is built on stilts on the flat roof.

The original plan was to cover the complete south oriented roof surface of the church building with photovoltaics; it was, however, rejected by the relevant monument protection authorities. The installation of two smaller and separated systems represents the compromise that was finally reached after long negotiations.

Location:	Dresden-Löbtau, Germany
Owner:	Katholische Pfarrei
	St. Antonius
Architect:	Schulze + Partner
Energy consultant:	Ingenieurbüro Dr. Scheffler &
	Partner GmbH
System provider:	Solarwatt
Year:	2001
Energy output:	3.45 kW$_p$
Energy yield:	2 900 kWh/a
Area:	26.5 m^2

Artilleriekaserne aus der Kaiserzeit *Osnabrück / Deutschland*

Das Projekt in Osnabrück ist ein Ergebnis des 1998 ins Leben gerufenen regionalen Aktionsprogramms Energieeinsparung / Solaroffensive (APES). Ziel des regionalen Förderprogramms ist die Finanzierung und Realisierung von Photovoltaikanlagen an landeseigenen Gebäuden in Niedersachsen. Jedes Einzelbeispiel soll die Möglichkeiten innovativer Solartechnik modellhaft nutzen und veranschaulichen.

Die unter Denkmalschutz stehende ehemalige Artilleriekaserne aus dem 19. Jahrhundert gehört dem Land Niedersachsen und wird von der Universität Osnabrück genutzt. Dazu wurde das Gebäude zum Hörsaal umgebaut und im Süddach eine Photovoltaikanlage installiert. Diese Anlage rief zunächst Einwände von denkmalpflegerischer Seite hervor: Man befürchtete, dass der authentische Gesamteindruck des aus heimischen Bruchsteinen gefertigten Baus geschädigt werden würde; zudem konnte das vorhandene Dachtragwerk nur wenige zusätzliche Lasten aufnehmen. Durch die Integration von Leichtbauelementen aus verzinktem Aluminium, auf die nanokristalline Dünnschicht-Solarzellen laminiert sind, konnte jedoch das Erscheinungsbild ebenso erhalten werden wie das filigrane Dachtragwerk.

Location:	Osnabrück, Germany
Owner:	Land Niedersachsen
Architect:	Planungsbüro Rohling AG
Energy consultant:	Decker & Mack
System provider:	ThyssenKrupp Solartec
Year:	2003
Energy output:	22.53 kW$_p$
Energy yield:	18 000 kWh/a
Area:	460 m^2

Former Imperial Artillery Barracks *Osnabrück / Germany*

The project in Osnabrück is a result of the regional Action Programme Energy Saving / *Solaroffensive* (APES), initiated in 1998. This regional funding programme aims to finance and implement photovoltaic installations on publicly owned buildings in the federal state of Niedersachsen. Each individual installation is intended to use and exemplify the possibilities of innovative solar technology.

The 19th century listed former artillery barracks building is the property of the federal state of Niedersachsen and is used by the University of Osnabrück. It was converted into a lecture hall and a photovoltaic system was installed on the south-facing roof. Initially, the monument protection authority had objections to the photovoltaic installation, as it wanted to preserve the authentic overall impression of the build-

ing, constructed from locally quarried stones. The existing roof structure was also incapable of supporting significant additional loads. The appearance of the building and the delicate roof supports were preserved by integrating light-weight construction elements made of galvanised aluminium, onto which the nano-crystalline thin-film solar cells are laminated.

„Deutsche Werkstätten" *Hellerau / Deutschland*

Das Gebäude-Ensemble der „Deutschen Werkstätten" in Hellerau am Rande von Dresden entstand in den Jahren 1909/10 als Fabrikneubau zur Produktion moderner Reformmöbel. Heute beherbergt der Werkstattkomplex ein Firmen- und Gründerzentrum. Volumen und Grundfläche des entbehrlich gewordenen Holzlagers werden jetzt von einem neuen Atelierhaus aufgenommen, das sich an die historische, denkmalgeschützte Steinmauer schmiegt.

Statt der Wiederherstellung des Ziegeldaches kam in Abstimmung mit der Denkmalschutzbehörde eine fortschrittliche Lösung in Form eines Solardachs zum Einsatz. Da für die Ateliernutzung direktes Sonnenlicht eher unerwünscht ist, bot sich die südorientierte Dachfläche für mehr Geschlossenheit und eine solare Stromerzeugung an.
Die polykristallinen Standard-Solarmodule bilden die wetterabweisende Dachhaut. Um der gestreckten Form des Gebäudes und dem

Raster der Steinmauer zu entsprechen, wurden sie horizontal gelagert und in ihren Maßen angepasst. Über einigen kleinen Fenstern, die ihre Luftzufuhr nur aus der Hinterlüftungsebene der Dachhaut erhalten, sind die entsprechenden Flächen in Glas ohne Photovoltaikzellen ausgeführt, so dass die Dachfläche optisch und konstruktiv einheitlich erhalten bleibt.

Location:	Dresden-Hellerau, Germany
Owner:	Grundbesitz Hellerau GmbH
Architect:	Peer Haller,
	Rudolf Morgenstern,
	Albrecht Quincke
Energy consultant:	SunStrom
System provider:	Solarwatt
Year:	2003
Energy output:	29.04 kW$_p$
Energy yield:	22 500 kWh/a
Area:	242 m^2

"Deutsche Werkstätten" *Hellerau / Germany*

The *Deutsche Werkstätten* (German Workshops) building ensemble was built as a factory producing modern furniture in Hellerau on the outskirts of Dresden in 1909/10. The factory complex now houses a business and entrepreneurial centre. The defunct wood-storage building has been replaced by a new atelier house with the same dimensions and floor area as the original, directly adjoining the historical, listed stone wall.

Instead of recreating the tiled roof, a progressive solution, in the form of a solar roof, was found in coordination with the monument preservation authority. As direct sunlight is undesirable for its use as an atelier, the south-facing roof surface was ideal for enabling both more compactness and solar power production.
The polycrystalline standard solar modules act as a weatherproof roof covering. They were installed horizontally and adjusted in size to

compliment the stretched shape of the building and the pattern of the stone wall. The glass surfaces directly above several small windows, which receive their air supply only via the rear ventilation level of the roofing, are installed without photovoltaic cells, preserving the optical and constructive unity of the roof surface.

Wohnanlage
Allington / England

Die Solardachlösung, die bei den *Gusto Homes* in Allington zur Anwendung kam, entspricht in Aussehen und Verhalten normalen Dachziegeln. Die photovoltaischen Dachelemente haben einen hohen Energieertrag und benötigen zur Gewinnung von 1 kW$_p$ weniger als 10 m^2 Fläche, sind also ideal geeignet für kleine Dachflächen.

Sie wurden zwar speziell für typische englische Dächer entwickelt, sind jedoch auch in anderen Ländern anwendbar. Sie können einfach und schnell auf Standardleisten montiert werden und lassen sich nahtlos zwischen die üblichen Dachziegel einfügen. Da sie dachintegriert sind, ersetzen sie konventionelle Produkte für die Dachdeckung, das heißt, sie übernehmen auch deren Funktion und stellen somit eine wirtschaftliche Lösung dar.

Sie sind gestalterisch unauffällig und eignen sich deshalb für Altbauten ebenso gut wie für Neubauten. Die gezeigte Wohnanlage wurde im alten Stil und mit traditionellen Materialien neu gebaut und steht hier stellvertretend als Beispiel für Altbauintegration.

Residential Estate
Allington / England

The solar roof installation used in the "Gusto Homes" in Allington corresponds in appearance and behaviour to normal roofing tiles. The photovoltaic roof elements have a high energy output and require less than 10 m^2 of space to produce 1 kW$_p$ which makes them ideally suited for small roof surfaces.

Although they were specially developed for typical British roofs, they can also be used in other countries. They can be quickly and easily mounted onto standard laths and inserted seamlessly between normal roof tiles. As they are integrated into the roof, they replace conventional roofing products, i.e. they also take over their function, thus presenting an economical solution.

Their design is inconspicuous, making them equally suitable for old and new buildings. The residential estate shown was newly built in the old style using traditional materials and is used here as an example of the integration of photovoltaics into old buildings.

Location:	Allington, England
Owner:	Steff Wright
Architect:	Gusto Homes
Energy consultant:	solarcentury
System provider:	solarcentury
Year:	2003
Energy output:	1 kW$_p$
Energy yield:	800 kWh/a
Area:	9.6 m^2

Gaubendächer *Bremen / Deutschland*

Im Rahmen des Dachausbaus des kleinen Reihenhauses aus den 1950er Jahren wurden zwei neue Gauben errichtet. Von Anfang an stand für den Bauherrn fest, dass er Solarenergie nutzen wollte; daher entschied er sich für eine Photovoltaikanlage.

Die um 20 Grad geneigten Dächer beider Gauben, die nach Südwesten bzw. Nordosten ausgerichtet sind, wurden mit Photovoltaik versehen. Die Einschätzung, dass aufgrund der Dachneigung nur unwesentlich geringere Energieerträge im Vergleich zu einer Anbringung in optimaler Süd-Ausrichtung erzielt werden könnten, hat sich inzwischen bestätigt.

Die Unterkonstruktion für die Photovoltaikanlage als Teil der Gauben wurde als regendichtes Dach mit Zellulosedämmung ausgeführt. Pro Gaube wurden 27 rahmenlose multikristalline Photovoltaikmodule mit einem universellen Befestigungssystem installiert. Das System hat die gleiche Bauhöhe wie die herkömmliche Dachdeckung, den Übergang bildet eine Edelstahlleiste. Auf den Gauben ersetzt die Photovoltaik die Dachziegel vollständig und ist ihnen in Regendichtigkeit und Sturmsicherheit gleichwertig. Die Standardmodule (je 53 cm x 120 cm) sind mit horizontalen Aluminiumprofilen und Vertikaldichtungen sicher eingefasst und gut hinterlüftet. Die Kabel sind geschützt in den Profilen verlegt.

Location:	Bremen, Germany
Owner:	Private
Energy consultant:	BUND
System provider:	Osmer solar
Year:	2003
Energy output:	4.3 kW$_p$
Energy yield:	3 250 kWh/a
Area:	34.9 m^2

Dormer Roofs *Bremen / Germany*

During the conversion of the attic of the small terraced-house from the 1950's, two new dormers were constructed. The building owner had decided from the beginning to use solar energy and chose to install a photovoltaic system.

The roofs of the two dormers, having an inclination of 20 degrees, oriented south-west and north-east respectively, were both equipped with photovoltaics. The judgement that energy gains would be possible that are only insignificantly smaller than in the case of an ideal south-orientation due to the inclination angle was confirmed in the meantime.

The sub-structure of the photovoltaic system is part of the dormer structure and has been realized as a rainproof roof with cellulose insulation. 27 frameless multicrystalline photovoltaic modules were installed on each dormer using an all-purpose fixing system. The system has the same installation height as the conventional roofing; the join is covered by a strip of stainless steel. The photovoltaic modules replace the roof tiles on the dormers completely and are their equals in terms of protection against rain and storms. The standard modules (53 cm x 120 cm each) are framed horizontally with aluminium profiles, sealed vertically and allow for ventilation behind them. The cabling is conducted in the profiles and is thus protected.

Location:	Meißen, Germany
Owner:	Evangelische Akademie Meißen
Architect:	Architekturbüro Pfau
Energy consultant:	Ingenieurbüro Dr. Scheffler & Partner GmbH
System provider:	SOLARWATT Solar-Systeme GmbH
Year:	2002/2003
Energy output:	2.76 kW$_p$
Energy yield:	2 300 kWh/a
Area:	21 m^2

Akademiegebäude „Alter Klosterhof" *Meißen / Deutschland*

Die Ursprünge des Augustinerklosters St. Afra reichen bis in das 13. Jahrhundert zurück. Es besteht aus mehreren Gebäudeteilen, welche schrittweise saniert wurden. Das denkmalgeschützte Gebäude-Ensemble wurde zu einer modernen Tagungs- und Begegnungsstätte (Evangelische Akademie) mit Beherbergungs- und Verpflegungsbetrieb umgewandelt. Durch Umbau und Anbauten wurden dem Ensemble neue Elemente als ablesbare weitere Schicht hinzugefügt. Die zurückhaltende Installation steht im Einklang mit der noch erhaltenen, behutsam sanierten historischen Bausubstanz.

Bei der Konzeption der technischen Anlage wurde besonderer Wert auf den Einsatz um-weltgerechter Technik und die Nutzung regenerativer Energien und Ressourcen gelegt. Ein mit Rapsöl betriebenes Blockheizkraftwerk versorgt das Ensemble mit Wärme und Strom. eine Regenwassernutzungsanlag speist die WC-Spülungen der Akademie mit dem Niederschlagswasser aller Dachflächen. Im Rahmen des weiteren Ausbaus wurden auf dem ältesten Gebäude, dem Kreuzganghaus, Solarwärme- und Solarstromanlagen errichtet.

Die netzgekoppelte Photovoltaikanlage wurde auf der Glasdachkonstruktion des neu errichteten Treppenturms installiert.

Die 24 semitransparent wirkenden Standard-module sind jeweils ca. 0,68 m x 1,30 m groß und bestehen aus schwarzen monokristallinen Zellen im Maß 10 cm x 10 cm. Sie haben eine Neigung von 8° und dienen gleichermaßen der Belichtung wie auch der Verschattung des darunterliegenden Treppenhauses. Gruppiert in drei Flächen zu je acht Modulen, verleihen sie der Anlage, die wie eine zusätzliche Überdachung wirkt, eine große optische Leichtigkeit. Zwischen den Modulflächen wurden Metallstege angebracht, um Zugänglichkeit und Wartung der Anlage zu gewährleisten.

Academy Building "Alter Klosterhof"   *Meißen / Germany*

The origins of the Augustinian monastery of St. Afra go back to the 13th century. It consists of several buildings, which have been renovated step by step. The group of listed buildings has been converted into a modern conference and meeting place (Lutheran Academy) with accommodation and catering facilities. New elements have been added to the ensemble in the course of the conversion and extension, as a visible new layer. The discreet installation harmonises with the carefully reconstructed historical architectural fabric.

The conception of the bulding services particularly emphasised the use of environmentally friendly technology, using regenerative energies and resources. A block heating and generating plant which runs on grapeseed oil provides heat and electricity for the academy. Rainwater collecting systems feed water gathered from all roof surfaces into the toilet cisterns in the buildings. Solar heating and electricity facilities were fitted in the oldest building, the cloisters house, as part of its further extension.

The grid-connected photovoltaic system was installed on the glass roof structure of the newly-built stair tower. The 24 semitransparent standard modules are each approx. 0.68 m x 1.30 m in size and made of black monocrystalline cells, each measuring 10 cm x 10 cm. They are installed at an 8° angle and provide both light and shade for the stairwell below. They were grouped in three lots of eight modules each, making the installation, which looks like an additional roof, appear very light. Metal footbridges were fixed between the module surfaces to enable easy access and maintenance to the system.

Kindermuseum *Rom / Italien*

Das Museum im historischen Stadtzentrum von Rom ist in einem ehemaligen Lagerhauskomplex für das Transportwesen untergebracht, das der Stadtverwaltung gehört. Die Hauptausstellungshalle ist eine Stahl- und Gusseisenkonstruktion aus dem Jahr 1920.

Beim Umbau sollten Raumklima und natürliche Belichtung verbessert und der Klimatisierungsbedarf reduziert werden. Es sollten nur Materialien zum Einsatz kommen, die recycelt sind bzw. recycelt werden können.

Die Installation einer Photovoltaikanlage geht auf den Vorschlag der Architekten zurück und fügte sich sehr gut in die pädagogische und ökologische Zielsetzung des Kindermuseums ein. Sie wurde teilweise über ein internationales Projekt im Rahmen des Thermie-Programms der Europäischen Kommission finanziert und als wesentliches architektonisches Gestaltungselement eingesetzt.

Die Photovoltaikinstallation ist in zwei unterschiedliche industrialisierte Systeme in Kombination mit Verschattungselementen und Oberlichtern gegliedert: ein 7 kW$_p$-System mit teils festen, teils beweglichen Vordachelementen an der Südfassade, und ein 8,2 kW$_p$-System als Dachintegration (transparente Glasmodule).

Die Gesamtanlage aus polykristallinen Siliziumzellen deckt 30 Prozent des Energiebedarfs für den Ausstellungsbetrieb und 60 Prozent der kompletten künstlichen Beleuchtung des Gebäudes. Aus Kostengründen wurden bei der Photovoltaikanlage nur Standardprodukte eingesetzt.

Das Oberlicht aus Isolierglas mit integrierten Photovoltaikmodulen wurde der vorhandenen Stahlkonstruktion angepasst. Beim Vordachsystem wurde der Einsatz der verschiebbaren Teile auf die Bereiche beschränkt, in denen das Raumklima und die natürliche Lichtqualität substantiell von dem Wechsel von Verschattung und Belichtung profitieren. Durch die Verschattung der Südfassade wurde der Raumkühlungsbedarf erheblich gesenkt.

Die Verkabelung für die Motoren wird offen gezeigt, so dass die Kinder den Weg, den der Strom nimmt, verfolgen können. Eine verspielte Installation im Gebäudeinneren zeigt den Kindern, wie viel Strom gerade erzeugt wird und was man damit alternativ betreiben könnte.

Location:	Rome, Italy
Owner:	Museo dei Bambini di Roma
Architect:	Studio Italplan
PV designer:	AeV Abbate e Vigevano Architetti
Energy consultant:	Gechelin Group
System provider:	Eurosolare
Year:	2001
Energy output:	15 kW$_p$
Energy yield:	18 8000 kWh/a
Area:	218 m^2

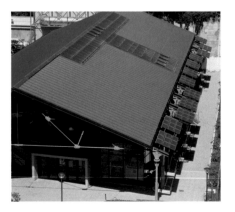

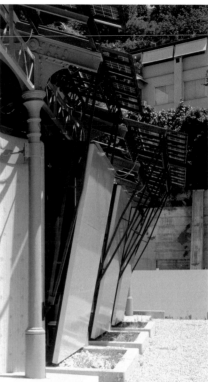

Children's Museum   *Rome / Italy*

The museum in the historic town centre of Rome is housed in a former complex of transport warehouses belonging to the local council. The main exhibition hall is a steel and cast iron structure dating back to 1920.

When the building was renovated and converted into a children's museum, indoor climate and natural lighting were to be improved and the need for air conditioning reduced. Moreover, only materials that were recycled and/or recyclable and non-toxic were to be used.

The installation of a photovoltaic system was originally proposed by the architects and it fitted in very well with the pedagogic and ecological objective of the museum. It was partially financed through an international project within the framework of the European Commission's "Thermie" programme and used as a fundamental architectural feature.

The photovoltaic installation is subdivided into two different industrialised systems in combination with shading elements and top lights: a 7 kW$_p$ system with some fixed and some moveable components on the canopy of the south façade and an 8.2 kW$_p$ system integrated into the roof (transparent glass modules). The entire system of polycrystalline silicon cells covers 30 percent of the energy requirement to run the exhibition and 60 percent of the whole artificial lighting of the building. For financial reasons, only standard products were used for the photovoltaic system.

The skylight, made of thermopane glazing with integrated photovoltaic modules, was adapted to the existing steel structure. For the moveable canopy system, the use of shiftable elements was restricted to areas where the indoor climate and the quality of natural light benefit substantially from the alternation of shade and light. Shading of the south façade reduces the cooling requirement considerably. The cabling for the motors is openly displayed so that the children can follow the path the electricity takes. A playful installation inside the building shows the children how much electricity is currently being generated and what could alternatively be operated by using it.

Kulturzentrum „Arena" *Berlin / Deutschland*

Das ursprüngliche Busdepot in Berlin-Treptow war im Jahr seiner Inbetriebnahme 1928 eine der größten freitragenden Hallen in Stahlskelettbauweise in Europa. Die denkmalgeschützte Halle mit einer stützenfreien Grundfläche von 6500 m² und einer Höhe von 12,50 m wird in einer Breite von 70 m von Trägern frei überspannt. Seit 1995 wird sie als Konzerthalle genutzt; Veranstaltungen mit bis zu 7500 Personen können heute darin stattfinden.

Bei der Vorbereitung der Sanierung im Jahr 1998 stimmten sich Architekt und Denkmalbehörde frühzeitig ab und trafen gemeinsam die Entscheidung, das Erscheinungsbild von 1928 nicht vollständig wiederherzustellen, sondern behutsam eine zeitgenössische Schicht hinzuzufügen. Das energetische Sanierungskonzept zielte darauf ab, die Anforderungen der gültigen Wärmeschutzverordnung noch um 20 Prozent zu übertreffen sowie Solarenergie zur

Stromerzeugung zu nutzen. Die Maßnahmen wurden durch das Berliner Umweltförderprogramm finanziell unterstützt.

Photovoltaik wurde in Form von monokristallinen Standardzellen jeweils auf einer Seite in die Verglasung der Lichtraupen des Daches integriert. Trotz der engen Zellabstände von 4 mm bzw. 12 mm ist aufgrund der einseitigen Anbringung und des breiten unbelegten Modulrandes eine gute Belichtung der Halle gewährleistet.

Da die Konstruktion der Lichtraupen erhalten blieb, wurde weder innen noch außen das Gesamterscheinungsbild verändert. Das originale Drahtglas der Lichtraupen konnte aus baurechtlichen Gründen (Anforderungen an Überkopfverglasung) nicht weiter verwendet werden, stattdessen wurde Ornamentglas als Verbundsicherheitsglas (VSG) eingebaut, das eine ähnliche Lichtstreuung erzielt.

Location:	Berlin, Germany
Owner:	Art Kombinat e.V.
	Kulturarena GmbH
Architect:	demel architekten
Energy consultant:	EnergieSystemTechnik
System provider:	Saint Gobain Glass
Year:	1999
Energy output:	30 kW$_p$
Energy yield:	620 kWh/a
Area:	209 m²

Performing Arts Facility "Arena"

Berlin / Germany

In 1928, the year it first began operating, the original bus depot in Berlin-Treptow was one of the largest cantilevered halls in Europe constructed with steel frames. The listed building has a floor area of 6,500 m² free of columns; at a height of 12.50 m, girders span a width of 70 m. Since 1995, it has been used as a concert hall; today events with up to 7,500 people can take place there. During preparation for renovation in 1998, the architect and the monument protection authority coordinated their requirements already in an early stage and took the joint decision not to completely restore the identity of the building of 1928, but to carefully add a contemporary layer.

The energy strategy of the renovation scheme aimed to save 20 percent more energy than required in accordance with the German Thermal Insulation Ordinance as valid at the time and to use solar energy for power generation. Financial support was provided by the Berlin environmental funding programme.

Photovoltaics in the form of monocrystalline standard cells were integrated into the glazing of the skylights on one side. Despite the narrow intervals between cells of 4 mm and 12 mm respectively, the installation of the cells on only one side of the skylights and the wide clear rim of the modules ensure that the hall is well lit.

Since the structure of the skylights was preserved, the overall appearance has remained unchanged both inside and outside. The original wired glass of the skylights could no longer be used because of planning and building laws and regulations (requirements regarding overhead glazing), so ornamental glass was used as laminated safety glass instead, which produces a similar effect in terms of light diffussion.

Haus „Lärche" *Braunwald / Schweiz*

Das Haus „Lärche" in Braunwald steht, nach Süden ausgerichtet, auf 1300 m ü. M. in den Glarner Alpen. Erbaut wurde es 1965 als Wohn- und Gästehaus der diakonischen Schwestern-schaft. Heute beherbergt es eine fünfköpfige Familie sowie ein Büro.

Der Bauzustand entsprach nicht mehr den heutigen Anforderungen; die kaum isolierte Gebäudehülle musste saniert und die veraltete Ölheizung ausgetauscht werden. Für die Bau-herren stand fest, dass bei dieser Gelegenheit ein umweltfreundliches Energiesystem instal-liert werden sollte. Die gut besonnte Lage so-wie Anforderungen wie Wintertauglichkeit und Wartungsfreundlichkeit führten zur Entschei-dung für den Einbau eines Solarluftsystems. Das Vorhaben wurde als Pilot- und Demons-trationsprojekt durch das schweizerische Bun-desamt für Energie finanziell unterstützt.

Das Dach wurde gedämmt; die nach Norden ausgerichteten Flächen wurden lediglich neu eingedeckt; das Süddach (ca. 75 m²) wurde mit einem Luftkollektorsystem ausgestattet, bei dem die anthrazitfarbene Blechdeckung der Absorber ist, während blendfreies Glas, mit Abstand dazu verlegt, die Dachhaut bildet. Das System nutzt die durch Sonneneinstrah-lung im Kollektor erwärmte Luft für Raumhei-zung und Wassererwärmung.

Das Vordach wurde mit einer semitranspa-renten Photovoltaikanlage eingedeckt, beste-hend aus acht Doppelglasmodulen mit grauen monokristallinen Zellen mit 1 cm Zellabstand. Neben der Stromerzeugung bieten die Modu-le den zusätzlichen Vorteil einer verbesserten Belichtung der Wohnräume.

Location:	Braunwald, Switzerland
Owner:	Markus & Margreth Hermann
Architect:	Markus Hermann
Energy consultant:	Amena
System provider:	BP solar
Year:	2000
Energy output:	1.6 kW$_p$
Energy yield:	1 500 kWh/a
Area:	15 m^2

"Lärche" House *Braunwald / Switzerland*

"Lärche" House in Braunwald is located at 1,300 m above sea level in the Glarner Alps, facing south. It was built as a residence and guest house of the Deaconess Sisterhood in 1965. Today it houses a family of five persons and a small office.

The state of the building structure did not correspond to modern requirements; the poorly insulated building shell had to be renovated and the obsolete oil heating system had to be exchanged. The owners were determined from the beginning to take the opportunity and to install an environmentally friendly energy system. The sunny location and the fact that the new system had to stand up to harsh winter weather and be easy to maintain, prompted them to install a solar air system. The project was supported financially by the Swiss Federal Energy Office.

The roof was insulated, the north-facing areas received new covering, while the south-facing roof (approx. 75 m^2) was equipped with a solar air collector system. Anthracite-coloured metal sheeting acts as an absorber, while the exterior roofing layer is formed by anti-glare glass, which is installed at a distance to the metal sheets. The system uses the air, which is heated in the collector by solar radiation, for room heating and hot water production.

The canopy of the front roof was covered with a semitransparent photovoltaic system, consisting of eight double-glass modules with grey monocrystalline cells at 1 cm intervals. As well as producing electricity, the modules offer the additional advantage of improved lighting for the rooms below.

Punkthäuser *Freiburg im Breisgau / Deutschland*

Da die beiden Wohngebäude in Freiburg im Breisgau aus den späten 1960er Jahren eine sehr schlechte Energiebilanz aufwiesen, entschloss sich die Eigentümerin, eine Baugenossenschaft, im Jahr 2001 zu einer Komplettsanierung inklusive Aufstockung durch ein zurückgesetztes Attikageschoss mit markantem Dachüberstand. Die Fassaden wurden gedämmt, Ost- und Westfassade mit neuen Zementfaserplatten versehen. Die Balkone wurden in Wintergärten umgewandelt.

Auf dem Dach eines der beiden Gebäude wurde eine solarthermische Anlage installiert, die 28 Prozent der Warmwasserversorgung für die Wohnanlage deckt.

Die geschlossenen Südfassaden wurden in voller Höhe mit einer Photovoltaikanlage versehen. Dafür wurde im Abstand von 20 cm vor die neue Dämmung eine hinterlüftete Fassadenschicht aus 190 cm breiten und 70 cm hohen Standardmodulen mit multikristallinen Solarzellen gehängt.

Der Stromertrag bei dieser vertikalen Anordnung ist etwa 25 Prozent geringer als bei einer optimal zur Sonne geneigten Solaranlage. Der mit der netzgekoppelten Anlage gewonnene Strom entspricht ca. 13 Prozent des Verbrauchs in den Gebäuden.

Location:	Freiburg, Germany
Owner:	Familienheim Freiburg Baugenossenschaft e.g.
Architect:	rolf + hotz
Energy consultant:	Stahl + Weiß
System provider:	Solarfabrik
Year:	2001
Energy output:	27 kW$_p$
Energy yield:	18 8000 kWh/a
Area:	230 m^2

Apartment Towers *Freiburg im Breisgau / Germany*

Due to the very poor energy balance of two 1960s residential buildings in Freiburg im Breisgau (Upper Rhine valley), the owner – a housing association – decided in 2001 to renovate the buildings entirely.

As part of the renovation work, a set-back penthouse level beneath prominent eaves was added, the building façades were insulated, cement fibre board siding was installed at the eastern and western façades and the balconies were converted into enclosed balconies.

A solar thermal system was installed on the roof of one of the two buildings and provides 28 percent of the warm water supply for the residential blocks.

A photovoltaic system was installed across the entire surface of the solid southern façades. This system is essentially a back-ventilated façade layer of standard modules (190 cm wide, 70 cm high) containing multicrystalline solar cells, which was installed at a distance of 20 cm from the new façade insulation.

This type of vertical solar system generates around 25 percent less power than a solar system that is tilted towards the sun at an optimum angle. The grid-connected photovoltaic system generates enough power to cover approx. 13 percent of the energy consumption of the buildings.

Location:	Delft, Netherlands
Owner:	Woonbron Delft
Architect:	Van Schagen architekten
Coordinator:	Delfts Energie Agentschap
Energy consultant:	W/E adviseurs
System provider:	BST Group
Year:	2003
Energy output:	26.4 kW$_p$
Energy yield:	17 800 kWh/a
Area:	260 m^2

Hochhaus *Delft / Niederlande*

Im Jahr 2003 wurde das älteste Hochhaus in Delft – erbaut im Jahr 1959 – komplett renoviert. Die Besitzerin, *Woningcorporatie Delftwonen* (heute: *Woonbron Delft*) beschloss die Nutzung von Solarenergie, um eine positive Umweltbilanz zu erreichen. Das Projekt ist Teil der Initiative „100 Delftblaue Dächer" der Stadt Delft, die von der Delfter Energie-Agentur DEA koordiniert wird.

An vier Gebäudeteilen wurde Photovoltaik unterschiedlicher Art und Größe installiert: an der Südfassade 104 Standardmodule mit je 55 polykristallinen Zellen; über dem Laubengang des

obersten Geschosses 38 Standardmodule mit je 60 polykristallinen Zellen; auf dem Dach des zugehörigen Flachbaus Kunststoffbahnen mit flexiblen Dünnschichtzellen auf 114 m^2; und an zwei Balkonbrüstungen je zwei großformatige Module mit jeweils 84 semitransparenten monokristallinen Zellen.

Drei der Installationen erfüllen weitere Aufgaben: Die Bewohner des obersten Geschosses kommen nun wettergeschützt zu den Wohnungen, der Belag auf dem Flachdach dient gleichzeitig der Abdichtung, und die Balkone haben einen semitransparenten Sichtschutz erhalten.

Das System ist netzgekoppelt und so ausgelegt, dass es den Strom für den Betrieb des Fahrstuhls, der mechanischen Lüftung und der Beleuchtung der Gemeinschaftsflächen liefert. Um den Demonstrationscharakter der Anlage zu unterstreichen, wird diese nachts weithin sichtbar beleuchtet.

Multi-Storey Building
Delft / Netherlands

In 2003 the oldest multi-storey building in Delft, built in 1959, was completely refurbished. The owner, *Woningcorporatie Delftwonen* (now: *Woonbron Delft*), decided on the use of solar energy to reach a positive environmental balance. The project is part of the "100 Delft blue roofs" initiative of the Delft municipality, which is coordinated by the Delft Energy Agency DEA.

Photovoltaic modules of different types and sizes were installed in four different parts of the building: 100 standard modules with 55 polycrystalline solar cells each on the south façade; 38 standard modules with 60 polycrystalline cells each above the access gallery of the top storey; flexible thin-film solar cells on synthetic waterproof material on 114 m^2 of the roof of the attached flat building; and two oversized modules with twice 84 semitransparent monocrystalline solar cells on each of the balustrades of two balconies.

Three of the four installations fulfil additional functions: The tenants of the top storey now have weather protected access to their apartments; the covering on the flat roof also serves as a sealed surface; and the balconies have now got a semitransparent sight protection.

The system is grid-connected and laid-out to produce and deliver the electricity for the elevator, the mechanical ventilation system and the lighting of the areas, which are jointly used by all tenants. The photovoltaic installation on the roof is lit up at night and visible from far away; this is meant to stress its demonstrative character.

Verwaltungsgebäude des Landeshochbauamtes *Feldkirch / Österreich*

Da das aus den 1960er Jahren stammende Verwaltungsgebäude in Feldkirch eine sehr schlechte Energiebilanz aufwies, entschied man sich Ende der 1990er Jahre für eine energetische Sanierung. Die Fenster wurden neu verglast, die Fassade wurde gedämmt und die Haustechnik erneuert. An der Südfassade wurde mittels einer Edelstahlkonstruktion und daran befestigter Jalousien ein Sonnenschutz für die dortigen Büroräume installiert. Da die Jalousien elektrisch betrieben werden, lag es nahe, Solarstrom dafür zu nutzen.

Als Zeichen für eine zukunftsorientierte Landespolitik stimmte die Landesregierung nach anfänglichen Bedenken hinsichtlich der Wirtschaftlichkeit schließlich dem Bau der Anlage zu. Die polykristallinen blauen Photovoltaikmodule mit dem Sondermaß 98,8 cm x 44,8 cm wurden, der Gebäudestruktur folgend, in die Edelstahlkonstruktion des Sonnenschutzes integriert und betonen die Vertikale. Die Farbigkeit der Module belebt die ansonsten sehr nüchterne Fassade.

Location:	Feldkirch, Austria
Owner:	Land Vorarlberg
Architect:	Landeshochbauamt Feldkirch
Energy consultant:	Landeshochbauamt Feldkirch
System provider:	stromaufwärts
Year:	1998
Energy output:	5.35 kW$_p$
Energy yield:	3 000 kWh/a
Area:	45 m^2

Administrative Office of the Building Surveyor's Office *Feldkirch / Austria*

In the late 1990s, due to the very poor energy balance of this administrative building in Feldkirch, which was built in the 1960s, it was decided that the building would have to undergo extensive renovation work. The windows got new glazing, the façade was insulated and the building services were renewed.

In order to provide sun protection for the south-facing offices, blinds, which are mounted onto a stainless steel construction, were added to the south façade. As the blinds are operated electrically, the use of solar power seemed the most logical step to take.

Following initial reservations concerning the cost-effectiveness of a solar power system, the government finally gave the project the go-ahead as a clear sign of its future-oriented politics.

The special-sized blue polycrystalline photovoltaic modules, which measure 98.8 cm x 44.8 cm each in accordance with the modular dimensions of the building, are integrated into the stainless steel sun shade construction and emphasise the vertical lines of the building. The colour of the modules livens up the rather austere design of the façade.

Appartementhaus *Aalborg / Dänemark*

Das *Yellow House* steht im Zentrum von Aalborg. Es wurde 1900 gebaut, hat vier Stockwerke und beherbergt acht Appartements. Die Fassaden sind nach Norden und Süden ausgerichtet mit der Südfassade zur Hofseite. 1996 wurde das Haus renoviert, um heutigen wie zukünftigen Standards zu entsprechen.

Die Fensterflächen wurden erheblich vergrößert, um bessere Belichtung zu gewährleisten; Isolierverglasung mit hohem Dämmwert und integrierten Sonnenschutzlamellen wurde eingebaut. Durch die Verglasung der Balkone wurde die Wohnfläche vergrößert. Das Lüftungssystem ist bedarfskontrolliert, um die Luftqualität im Gebäudeinneren zu verbessern und den mechanischen Lüftungsaufwand zu verringern. Die Warmwasserversorgung erfolgt zu ca. 30 Prozent über in das Dach integrierte Solarkollektoren.

An der Südfassade wurden hinterlüftete Photovoltaikmodule angebracht. Einige von ihnen sind 30 Grad gegen die Vertikale geneigt, aber die meisten von ihnen sind vertikal angebracht. Diese Art der Integration mindert zwar die Energieausbeute aufgrund der zusätzlichen Glasschicht und der geringeren direkten Sonneneinstrahlung im Vergleich zu geneigten Modulen, dennoch sprachen nicht nur architektonische, sondern auch technische Gründe für diese Realisierung: Die Photovoltaikmodule können so als Absorber in der Hinterlüftung der Solarwände dienen und verleihen der Fassade ihr besonderes Aussehen.

Wenn der Stromverbrauch im Haus geringer ist als die produzierte Strommenge, wird der Energieüberschuss gegen Vergütung in das Stromnetz eingespeist.

Apartment Building *Aalborg / Denmark*

The four-storey "Yellow House" in the centre of Aalborg was built in 1900 and houses eight apartments. The façades face north and south, with the south-facing façade at the back of the building. The house was refurbished in 1996 in order to conform to current and future standards.

The window surfaces were made considerably larger to guarantee better lighting; new glazing with a high insulating level and integrated solar protection slats was installed. Residential space was extended through the glazing of the balconies. The ventilation system is controlled according to current requirements, improving the air quality in the interior of the building and reducing the need for mechanical ventilation. Solar collectors that provide approximately 30 percent of the hot water supply are integrated into the roof.

Rear ventilated photovoltaic modules were mounted on the south-facing façade. A number of these are slanted at a 30 degree angle, but most are mounted vertically. This type of wall integration reduces the energy yield, due to the additional glass layer and the lower level of direct solar radiation compared to tilted modules. It was carried out in this way for both architectural and technical reasons (the photovoltaic modules act as absorbers in the rear ventilation of the solar walls) and gives the façade a unique appearance.

When less electricity is consumed in the building than the system produces, the surplus energy is fed into the grid in return for payment.

Location:	Aalborg, Denmark
Owner:	Municipality of Aalborg
Architect:	Jacob Blegvad
Energy consultant:	Esbensen Consulting Engineers
System provider:	GAIA Solar
Year:	1996
Energy output:	2.8 kW$_p$
Energy yield:	700 kWh/a
Area:	22 m^2

Karren-Seilbahn *Dornbirn / Österreich*

1956 wurde die erste kleine Pendelbahn auf den Karren, den Hausberg der Stadt Dornbirn, gebaut; 1995/96 wurde die Bahn und im Zusammenhang damit auch die Bergstation saniert und erweitert. Die Bergstation bekam eine Fassadenisolierung und eine neue Heizung und wurde durch den Anbau eines Aussichtsrestaurants mit Kiosk und Mitarbeiterquartieren erweitert.

Die Stadt Dornbirn bemüht sich um den Einsatz ressourcenschonender und umweltverträglicher Energiegewinnung und entschloss sich deshalb in ihrer Funktion als Eigentümerin der Seilbahn zusammen mit deren Betreiber, eine Photovoltaikanlage am Gebäude zu installieren. Diese ist als kleines Demonstrationsprojekt, besonders für Schulklassen und vorbeikommende Wanderer, konzipiert; deshalb wurden auch sichtbare Datenableseeinrichtungen montiert, um Produktion und Wirtschaftlichkeit der Photovoltaikanlage einer breiten Öffentlichkeit verständlich zu machen.

Die Idee zur Solaranlage entstand allerdings erst nach Fertigstellung des Anbaus, so dass eine direkte Integration der Module in die Fassade nicht mehr möglich war. Stattdessen wurde vor die sanierte Südfassade mit 10 cm Abstand ein Streifen aus 16 kristallinen Standardmodulen (0,65 m x 1,00 m) unter die Fenster gesetzt, sowie ein weiterer identischer Streifen über die Fenster des Anbaus.

Location:	Dornbirn, Austria
Owner:	Municipality of Dornbirn
Architect:	Leopold Kaufmann
Energy consultant:	stromaufwärts
System provider:	stromaufwärts
Year:	1996
Energy output:	2.65 kW$_p$
Energy yield:	700 kWh/a
Area:	21 m^2

Karren Cable Car   *Dornbirn / Austria*

In 1956, the first small cable car on the Karren, the local mountain of Dornbirn, was built. In 1995/96, the cable car and also the summit station were refurbished and extended. The summit station now has façade insulation and new heating and a panorama restaurant with a kiosk and accommodation for staff has been added as an extension.

The municipality of Dornbirn endeavours to use resource-saving and environmentally compatible energy production and so, as owner of the cable car system, decided together with the operators of the railway to install photovoltaic equipment on the building. This is designed as a small demonstration project particularly for school classes and passing hikers. Consequently, meters with information for the general public about the production and economic efficiency of the photovoltaic facility have been installed in prominent positions.

Since the idea of a solar facility was conceived only after the extension had been completed, it was no longer possible to integrate the modules directly into the façade. Instead, a strip of 16 crystalline standard modules (0.65 m x 1.00 m) was mounted below the windows in front of the renovated south façade, at a distance of 10 cm, and a further identical strip was mounted above the windows of the extension.

Verwaltungsgebäude der Stadtwerke *Aachen / Deutschland*

Als das Energie- und Wasserversorgungsunternehmen STAWAG (Stadtwerke Aachen AG) 1991 sein aus den 1960er Jahren stammendes Verwaltungsgebäude sanierte, lag es für den Architekten nahe, im Rahmen der energetischen Sanierung eine Photovoltaikanlage in die Glasfassade des Treppenhauses zu integrieren.

Zum ersten Mal weltweit wurden hierfür Module entwickelt, bei denen Solarzellen in Isolierglas (Verbundscheiben) eingebettet sind. Zwischen die Scheiben des äußeren Verbundes sind die Solarzellen eingebettet, zwischen die des inneren Verbundes ist eine lichtstreuende Folie einlaminiert. Die insgesamt 103 Solarmodule wurden dem Fassadenraster entsprechend maßgefertigt und wechseln sich in der Fassade mit Fensterflächen ab. Die gesamte Verkabelung ist in die Rahmen der Metallfassade integriert. Die solare Südfassade hat nun guten Wärmeschutz und den Doppelnutzen von Stromerzeugung zur Netzeinspeisung und Sonnenschutz für den dahinter liegenden Raum.

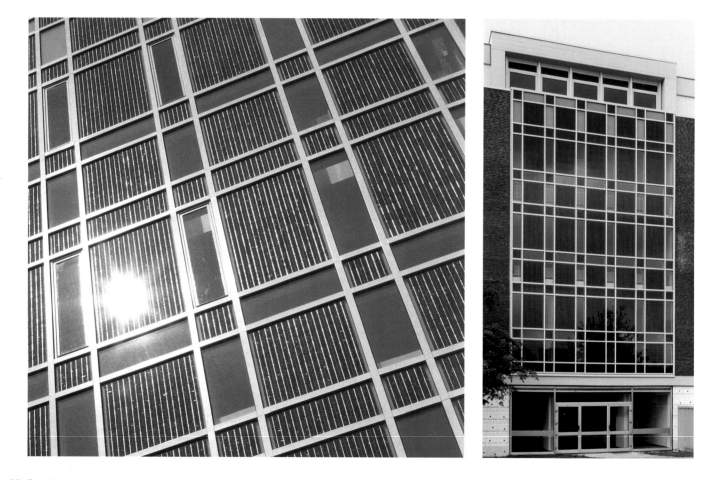

Public Utilities Administrative Building *Aachen / Germany*

In 1991, when the Aachen municipal utility, the *Stadtwerke Aachen AG* (STAWAG), began renovation work on its 1960s administrative building, the idea of installing a photovoltaic system in the glass façade of the stairwell suggested itself to the architects.

For the first time anywhere in the world, modules were developed in which solar cells were embedded within insulation glass (compound construction). The solar cells are embedded between the outer panes, while a special foil is placed between the inner panes to diffuse incident light.

A total of 103 photovoltaic modules were custom-made to correspond with the existing segmentation of the building façade and they alternate with window areas in the composition of the façade. The cabling is completely integrated into the metal frames of the façade.

The solar system in the south façade now provides good heat insulation, generates electricity that is fed into the power grid and also provides sun protection for the spaces behind it.

Location:	Aachen, Germany
Owner:	STAWAG Stadtwerke
Architect:	Georg Feinhals
Energy consultant:	STAWAG Stadtwerke
System provider:	FLABEG Solar International
Year:	1991
Energy output:	4.2 kW$_p$
Energy yield:	3 200 kWh/a
Area:	37 m^2

Touristeninformation in Kirchenruine
Alès / Frankreich

Die Touristeninformation von Alès ließ sich in der Ruine einer Kirche aus dem 16. Jahrhundert in der Innenstadt nieder. Vom ursprünglichen Gebäude sind nur der Glockenturm und ein Teil des Längsschiffs erhalten, an dessen Außenwand sich drei große Mauerbögen von jeweils dreizehn Metern Höhe, sechs Metern Breite und drei Metern Tiefe befinden.

Der Architekt schlug eine zusätzlichen Raum gewinnende Lösung vor: Drei von einer Metallstruktur getragene auskragende Baukörper beherbergen nun die Büros. Da sie zur Südseite liegen und sehr exponiert sind, war ein Sonnen- und Sichtschutz erforderlich; man entschied sich für eine Photovoltaikintegration, um die Sonneneinstrahlung sinnvoll zu nutzen. Die drei vorgehängten Fassaden bestehen aus jeweils 70 nach Süden und Südosten ausgerichteten Photovoltaikmodulen in der Größe von jeweils 47,5 cm x 101 cm. Die verwendeten Solarzellen wurden mit ihrem bräunlichen Farbton dem Kalkstein der Ruine speziell angepasst. Durch den Abstand zwischen den Zellen sind die Module semitransparent und lassen Tageslicht in den Innenraum. Die gesamte Verkabelung wird unsichtbar in der vertikalen Metallstruktur geführt. Hierfür wurde ein spezieller Anschluss an den Seiten der Module entwickelt. Der gewonnene Strom wird in das Netz eingespeist.

Um einen idealen klimatischen Austausch zwischen den beiden Konstruktionen – dem alten Gebäudeteil mit sehr massiven Wänden und dem Photovoltaiksystem – zu schaffen, wurde die Photovoltaikfassade hinterlüftet vor die Isolierglasschicht gesetzt und mit einem Ventilatorsystem gekoppelt. Dieses System ist mit einer autonomen Luftdurchflusskontrolle und Temperaturfühlern ausgestattet. Im Sommer wird die Stauwärme hinter der Photovoltaikfassade von den Ventilatoren nach außen abgeführt und Frischluft wird angesaugt; im Winter wird sie von den Ventilatoren zur Beheizung in den alten, kühleren Gebäudeteil geleitet.

Tourist Information Bureau in Church Ruins *Alès / France*

The tourism office of Alès is located in the ruins of a 16th century church in the centre of the town. Only the bell tower and part of the nave have survived, with three large stone arches measuring thirteen metres high, six metres wide and three metres deep on the outer wall. The architect suggested a solution aimed at creating additional space: Three cantilevered volumes supported by a metal structure now house the offices. As they face south and are very exposed, they required protection from the sun and from prying eyes; the solution was a photovoltaic integration, in order to make the best use of the solar radiation.

Each of the three curtain wall façades consists of seventy 47.5 cm x 101 cm south- and south-east-facing photovoltaic modules. The brown solar cells used were especially adapted to match the colour of the limestone material of the church. The modules are semitransparent due to the interspaces between the cells, allowing daylight into the interior of the building. All electrical cables are integrated invisibly into the vertical metal structure, using a specially developed connection on the sides of the modules. The electricity generated is fed into the grid.

To achieve an ideal climatic exchange between the two structures – the old building with very massive walls and the photovoltaic system – the photovoltaic façade has been set at distance in front of the thermopane glass windows and coupled with a ventilation system. The latter includes an autonomous airflow-rate control and temperature sensors. In summer the ventilators channel the heat, which builds up behind the photovoltaic façade, to the outside, while fresh air is drawn in; in winter the heat is conducted into the old part of the building where it is used for room heating.

Location:	Alès, France
Owner:	Ville d'Alès
Architect:	Jean-François Rougé
Energy consultant:	SOLARTE
System provider:	Photowatt
Year:	2001
Energy output:	9.5 kW$_p$
Energy yield:	6 500 kWh/a
Area:	100 m^2

„Kollektivhuset" *Kopenhagen / Dänemark*

Das *Kollektivhuset*, ein Wohnhaus für behinderte Menschen in Kopenhagen, ist ein typischer Betonbau aus den späten 1950er Jahren mit 11 Geschossen. Die nach Westen auf eine stark befahrene Straße gerichtete Fassade bestand ursprünglich aus offenen Balkonen mit repetitivem Charakter. Im Zuge der Umgestaltung im Jahr 2002 wurden die Balkone durch Entfernen der alten Brüstungen und eine Verglasung in einer vorgehängten Edelstahlkonstruktion größer, komfortabler und besser zugänglich gemacht.

In die neue Glasfassade wurde auf Brüstungsebene eine Photovoltaikanlage integriert. Hinter den Modulen ist an der Innenseite ein flexibles System von beweglichen Platten angebracht, die sich im selben Rahmen wie das Glas verschieben lassen. Dieses System dient der individuellen Nutzung der Stauwärme, die sich hinter den Modulen bildet: Im Sommer kann die Wärme nach außen abgeleitet werden, indem die Platte direkt hinter das Photovoltaikmodul geschoben wird; im Winter, wenn die Wärme im verglasten Balkon genutzt werden soll, wird die Platte einfach zur Seite geschoben.

Heute hat die Fassade ein sehr viel abwechslungsreicheres Erscheinungsbild als früher: Reflektierende und geöffnete Glasflächen und die Komposition aus verschiedenfarbigen Glasscheiben hinter den Solarmodulen ergeben ein Bild der wechselnden Nutzung der Balkone. Die horizontalen und vertikalen Elemente der Fassade werden außerdem in wechselndem Licht und zu verschiedenen Jahreszeiten unterschiedlich betont.

In der Eingangshalle des Gebäudes wurde eine Anzeigentafel aufgestellt, welche jeweils die von der Photovoltaikanlage momentan und seit Inbetriebnahme erzeugte akkumulierte Strommenge anzeigt. Auf diese Weise können die Mieter den Nutzen des in ihrer Wohnung installierten Systems konkret nachvollziehen.

Location:	Copenhagen, Denmark
Owner:	Vanføres Boligselskab
	Københavns Kommune
Architect:	Domus Arkitekter
Energy Consultant:	Esbensen Consulting Engineers
System Provider:	Gaia Solar
Year:	2002
Energy Output:	12 kW$_p$
Energy yield:	4 500 kWh/a
Area:	166 m^2

"Kollektivhuset" *Copenhagen / Denmark*

The *Kollektivhuset*, a residential building for disabled people in Copenhagen, is a typical late 1950s concrete construction with 11 storeys. The west-facing façade looks toward a busy street and originally featured repetitively placed open balconies. During its redesigning in 2002 the balconies were made larger, more comfortable and more easily to access. This was achieved by removing the old balustrades and enclosing the balcony in a suspended high-grade steel and glass structure.

A photovoltaic system was integrated into the new glass façade at the balustrade level. Behind the modules, a flexible system of move-able plates is mounted on the interior side that can be slid across within the same framework as the glass. Depending on the season, this system makes specific use of the stored heat that builds up behind the modules. In the summer, sliding the plate directly behind the photovoltaic module can channel this heat outside; in the winter, when the heat in the glazed balcony can be put to good use, the plate is simply slid aside.

The new façade has a far more interesting and varied appearance compared to its predecessor: reflecting and opened glass surfaces and the composition of differently coloured glass panes behind the solar modules create a picture of the varying use of the balconies. The horizontal and vertical elements of the façades are also differently emphasised in changing light conditions and different seasons.

A display panel has been installed in the enttrance hall of the building, showing the current output of the photovoltaic system and the total amount of generated electricity accumulated since ist was started up. This helps the tenants to understand the benefits of the system installed in their apartments in concrete terms.

Energie-Forschungszentrum *Petten / Niederlande*

Das Bürogebäude des Niederländischen Energie-Forschungszentrums (ECN) in Petten, Baujahr 1963, wies grundlegende technische und klimatische Mängel auf, die durch die Renovierung im Jahr 2001 behoben wurden. Da die Fassade im Sommer immer überhitzt war, wurde auch ein außenliegender Sonnenschutz vorgesehen, der eine teure und Energie verbrauchende Klimaanlage überflüssig macht.
Die Photovoltaikanlage wurde in den Sonnenschutz integriert; durch diese Integration und den Verzicht auf ein konventionelles Photovoltaik-Montagesystem konnten die Baukosten optimiert werden.
In Anbetracht der hohen Kosten eines beweglichen, das heißt dem Einstrahlungswinkel der Sonne nachgeführten Systems und des nur geringfügig höheren Energiegewinns gegenüber einem feststehenden System, entschied man sich für eine im idealen Winkel angebrachte, 37 Grad gegen die Horizontale geneigte Lamellenstruktur. Die Länge der Lamellen wurde mit 3 m auf das Gebäuderaster abgestimmt. Jede der 84 cm breiten Lamellen trägt drei Module mit je 36 in Glas eingebetteten Solarzellen.
Um einfache Instandhaltung, Zugänglichkeit und Fensterreinigung zu ermöglichen, wurde der gesamte Sonnenschutz als weitere Fassadenschicht ca. 80 cm vor das Gebäude gestellt.

Energy Research Centre *Petten / Netherlands*

Built in 1963, the premises of the Energy research Centre of the Netherlands (ECN) in Petten, displayed fundamental technical and climatic shortcomings which were rectified during the renovation work in 2001. As the façade was constantly overheated in the summer months, a sun protection system was installed on the outside of the building, thus dispensing with the need for a costly and energy consuming air-conditioning system.

The photovoltaic system was integrated into the sun protection system. Owing to this fact, as well as the decision to forgo the use of a conventional photovoltaic mounting system, construction costs could be optimised.

As an adjustable solar system, i.e. with sun-tracking solar panels, is both expensive and does not collect much more energy than a solar system with fixed modules, a slat structure tilted at an ideal angle of 37 degrees to the horizontal was opted for. Slats of 3 metres in length were used in order to comply with the modular dimensions of the building. Each of the slats, which are 84 cm in width, holds three modules containing 36 glass-embedded solar cells each.

In order to allow for easy maintenance, accessibility and window cleaning, the entire sun protection system was installed over the existing building façade as an additional façade layer with a clearance of approximately 80 cm.

Location:	Petten, Netherlands
Owner:	Netherlands Energy Research Foundation
Architect:	BEAR Architecten
Energy consultant:	ECN & Shell Solar
System provider:	Shell Solar
Year:	2001
Energy output:	26.21 kW$_p$
Energy yield:	20 000 kWh/a
Area:	262 m^2

Redaktionsgebäude
Albstadt-Ebingen / Deutschland

Da die architektonische Erscheinung des Redaktionsgebäudes des Zollern-Alb-Kuriers weder der lokalen Bedeutung der Tageszeitung noch der seiner städtischen Lage entsprach, entschloß sich der Eigentümer, das Gebäude von 1973 komplett zu sanieren, zumal eine energetische Berechnung ergab, dass sich eine Sanierung auch aus gebäudewirtschaftlichen Gründen lohnen würde.

Im Zuge der Sanierung wurden die vorhandenen Fenster und die Stahlbetonfensterbrüstungen der Südseite gegen raumhohe Fenster ausgetauscht und mit einem aktiven Sonnenschutz in Form von mit Photovoltaik bestückten Glaslamellen versehen. Auf diese Weise wird eine zu starke Aufheizung der Räume verhindert, so dass keine Klimatisierung benötigt wird. Gleichzeitig produziert die Verschattungseinrichtung nutzbare elektrische Energie. Die Lamellen richten sich selbsttätig nach dem Sonnenstand.

Die Konstruktion von Traggerüst und Antriebselementen der vorgesetzten Fassade ist technisch raffiniert und gleichzeitig unauffällig. Die im Abstand von ca. 50 cm vor die bisherige Fassade gehängten Solarlamellen haben ein Modulmaß von 55 cm x 168 cm, sind der Größe der Fenster angepasst und mit semitransparenten kristallinen Solarzellen in der Standardgröße 10 cm x 10 cm bestückt.

Mit seiner offen gezeigten Technik nimmt sich das Gebäude zwischen einem Fachwerk-Neubau und dem unsanierten Pendant eigenständig und zeitgemäß aus.

Editing Office

Albstadt-Ebingen / Germany

As the architectural appearance of this office building of the *Zollern-Alb-Kurier*, dating back to 1973, failed to convey either the significance of the daily paper or its prime location, the owner decided to completely overhaul it. Especially since an in-depth energy assessment showed that the renovation would also be worthwhile in economic terms.

During the renovation work, the existing windows and reinforced concrete window parapets on the south side were replaced by floor to ceiling windows covered with an active sun shade in the form of glass slats containing photovoltaic elements. This prevents the rooms from overheating, thus dispensing with the need for air conditioning; at the same time the sun protection system produces useable electrical energy. The slats adjust themselves automatically, depending on the position of the sun.

The construction of the supporting structure and drive elements of the suspended façade are both sophisticated in technical terms and at the same time subtle in design. The solar slats, hung approximately 50 cm in front of the existing façade, have modular dimensions of 55 cm x 168 cm, are adapted to the size of the windows and contain standard 10 cm x 10 cm, semitransparent crystalline solar cells.

With its new, openly displayed technology, the building looks both self-sufficient and modern between its pre-renovated counterpart and a new half-timbered style building.

Location:	Albstadt, Germany
Owner:	Zollern-Alb-Kurier
Architect:	Friedrich Rau, Axel Schlueter
Energy consultant:	Delzer Kybernetik
System provider:	PHP Glastec-Systeme
Year:	2004
Energy output:	4.3 kW$_p$
Energy yield:	4 500 kWh/a
Area:	84 m^2

Solare Informationstafel *La Spezia / Italien* PVACCEPT-Demonstrationsanlage

In der denkmalgeschützten Festungsanlage *Castello San Giorgio* in La Spezia ist ein archäologisches Museum untergebracht. Das ursprüngliche Informationsbanner des Museums neben dem Eingang wurde durch eine Informationstafel ersetzt, die aus sechs übergroßen (1,20 m x 1,20 m) Photovoltaikmodulen in Dünnschichttechnologie besteht. Die von PVACCEPT entwickelte innovative Idee, die Module mit einem gleichmäßigen Punktraster in wetterbeständigem keramischem Siebdruck zu versehen, wurde hier zum ersten Mal angewendet. Das originale Design des Museumsbanners wurde dabei übernommen und gestalterisch neu interpretiert.

Die 2,40 m x 3,60 m große Anlage ist mit nur wenigen Haltepunkten in ca. 10 cm Abstand vor der Festungsmauer montiert, um die Eingriffe in das historische Gemäuer, wie mit der zuständigen Denkmalschutzbehörde abgestimmt, möglichst gering zu halten. Die minimierte selbsttragende Konstruktion aus Stahl- und Aluminiumprofilen ist eine Spezialanfertigung.

Der von der Anlage erzeugte Strom wird in einer in der Eingangshalle des Museums untergebrachten Batterie gespeichert und dazu genutzt, einen neu angebrachten, im Boden eingelassenen, energiesparenden Strahler zu speisen, der die Informationstafel nachts beleuchtet.

Die 2004 errichtete Anlage ist mit einem automatischen System ausgestattet, das Energieerzeugung und -verbrauch misst und von dem die Daten jederzeit zur Kontrolle abgerufen werden können.

Location:	La Spezia, Italy
Owner:	Comune di La Spezia
Architect:	PVACCEPT / UdK Berlin
Energy consultant:	PVACCEPT / BUSI IMPIANTI
System provider:	PVACCEPT / Würth Solar
Year:	2004
Energy output:	720 W_p
Energy yield:	350 kWh/a
Area:	8.6 m^2

Solar Information Board   *La Spezia / Italy*   PVACCEPT Demonstration Object

The monument castle *San Giorgio* in La Spezia houses an archaeological museum. The original museum information banner, which sat beside the entrance, was replaced with a board consisting of six oversized (1.20 m x 1.20 m) thin-film photovoltaic modules. The innovative idea of screen-printing an even matrix of dots onto the modules using weather resistant ceramic colour was developed by PVACCEPT and applied here for the first time. The original design of the museum information banner was adopted and aesthetically re-interpreted.

The installation has a size of 2.40 m x 3.60 m. The board is fixed to the castle wall at very few points and with approximately 10 cm distance from the wall. In this way, the historical masonry is impacted upon as little as possible, as was stipulated by the relevant monument protection authority. The minimal self-supporting structure, comprising steel and aluminium sections, is a custom-made design.

The power generated by the solar panels is stored in a battery located in the entrance hall of the museum and used to operate a newly installed, energy saving spotlight in the ground that illuminates the information board at night. The installation, erected in 2004, is equipped with an automatic data logging system that measures power generation and consumption and can be used to call up and check data at any time.

Schillerzitat-Tafel an der Stadtmauer
Marbach am Neckar / Deutschland
PVACCEPT-Demonstrationsanlage

An der historischen Stadtmauer in Marbach am Neckar wurde in Abstimmung mit der zuständigen Denkmalpflegebehörde eine aus neun übergroßen (1,20 m x 1,20 m) Dünnschichtmodulen bestehende Solartafel angebracht. Diese wurden mit derselben Technik, die auch beim Projekt in La Spezia angewandt wurde, durch Bedruckung farbig gestaltet. Zur optischen Anpassung an die historische Natursteinmauer wurden deren Struktur und Farbigkeit als Hintergrund auf die Module übertragen. Das Grundmuster ist bei allen neun Modulen gleich. Die Tragkonstruktion aus Aluminiumprofilen ist eine Spezialanfertigung; der Abstand zwischen den Modulen und der Mauer beträgt ca. 15 cm, was eine gute Hinterlüftung garantiert.

In der Mitte der 3,60 m x 3,60 m großen Tafel wurde ein Zitat von Friedrich Schiller, dessen Geburtsstadt Marbach am Neckar ist, hinzugefügt. Das von der Gemeinde ausgewählte Zitat „Der gebildete Mensch macht die Natur zu seinem Freund" stellt den Bezug zur umwelt- und ressourcenschonenden Energieerzeugung der Solartechnik her.

Die 2004 errichtete Anlage ist mit einem automatischen System ausgestattet, das Energieerzeugung und -verbrauch misst und von dem die Daten jederzeit zur Kontrolle abgerufen werden können.

Solar Quotation Board at City Wall   *Marbach am Neckar / Germany*   PVACCEPT-Demonstration Object

In agreement with the relevant monument protection authority, a solar board, comprising nine oversized (1.20 m x 1.20 m) thin-film modules, was mounted onto the historical city wall of Marbach am Neckar. The same method of module colour design that was used in the project in La Spezia, Italy, was also applied in this project. To ensure optical harmony with the natural stone of the historical city wall, the structure and colours of the wall were adopted as background design for the modules. The basic pattern of all nine modules is identical.

The board is supported by a custom-made structure comprising aluminium profiles. The distance between the modules and the wall surface is approximately 15 cm, thus ensuring sufficient ventilation behind the modules. Additionally, the centre of the 3.60 m x 3.60 m board bears a quotation from Friedrich Schiller, who was born in Marbach am Neckar. The quotation, which was chosen by communal representatives – *Der gebildete Mensch macht die Natur zu seinem Freund* (English: "An educated man takes nature as his friend") –

concurs with the environmentally friendly, resource saving solar technology.

The installation, erected in 2004, is equipped with an automatic data logging system that measures power generation and consumption and can be used to call up and check data at any time.

Location:	Marbach / Neckar, Germany
Owner:	Stadt Marbach am Neckar
Architect:	PVACCEPT / UdK Berlin
Energy consultant:	PVACCEPT / Würth Solar
System provider:	PVACCEPT / Würth Solar
Year:	2004
Energy output:	1 080 W_p
Energy yield:	600 kWh/a
Area:	13 m^2

„Sonnenfalle"
Hochschule für bildende Künste
Hamburg / Deutschland

Die Lage der seit 1999 existierenden konventionellen Photovoltaikanlage auf dem Flachdach des Gebäudes der Hochschule für bildende Künste in Hamburg ist wenig öffentlichkeitswirksam, weshalb der Wunsch entstand, dieser großen (Leistung: 10 kW$_p$), aber unscheinbaren Anlage eine auffälligere und weithin sichtbare „kleine Schwester" an die Seite zu stellen. Diese sollte dazu beitragen, die Kunsthochschule als Ort künstlerisch-technischen Experimentierens öffentlich darzustellen.

1998 wurde deshalb ein studentischer Realisierungswettbewerb ausgelobt, der ausdrücklich einen künstlerisch-konzeptionellen Anspruch für die geplante neue Photovoltaikanlage (Leistung: 2 kW$_p$) formulierte. Die Jury entschied sich für die Realisierung der „Sonnenfalle" und sah in diesem Entwurf die Intention des Wettbewerbes überzeugend getroffen.

Für die Anlage wurden multikristalline Solarzellen mit größeren Abständen als technisch erforderlich in Glas eingebettet, wobei zum ersten Mal Hinterschnittdübel in Glas als Befestigung verwendet wurden (drei Stück pro Modul im Rückglas aus 10 mm dickem Floatglas). Insgesamt 64 der leicht, transparent und schwebend wirkenden Module mit einer Größe von 41 cm x 81 cm wurden auf eine gebogene, vor die Fassade gesetzte und bis über das Dach reichende Stahlrohrkonstruktion montiert.

"Sun Trap" ("Sonnenfalle") at College of Fine Arts

Hamburg / Germany

The conventional photovoltaic system installed at the College of Fine Arts in Hamburg, which has existed since 1999, does not attract much public attention due to its location on the flat roof of the college building. For precisely this reason, it was decided to give this rather powerful (10 kW_p), yet inconspicuous photovoltaic system a more noticeable and visible "little sister", the aim of which was to help portray the art school to the public as a place of artistic and technical experimentation.

In 1998 a design competition was held in which students were asked to come up with an artistic design concept for the new photovoltaic system (power rating: 2 kW_p). The prize went to the *Sonnenfalle*, a design concept that convincingly fulfilled the intention of the competition.

The new photovoltaic system comprises multicrystalline solar cells, which were set apart at larger distances than actually required for technical reasons and embedded in glass. And, for the first time ever, undercut anchors in glass were used to fix the system (3 per module in the back of 10-mm-thick float glass). A total of 64 lightweight, transparent modules (41 cm x 81 cm each) which appear to be "hovering" were mounted onto an arched steel pipe structure and fitted onto the building façade, the tops of the structure extending even beyond the rooftop.

Location:	Hamburg, Germany
Owner:	Hochschule für bildende Künste
Architects:	Händle, Niemeyer, Rieper
Energy consultant:	solarnova
System provider:	solarnova
Year:	1998
Energy output:	2 kW_p
Energy yield:	1 600 kWh/a
Area:	21.3 m^2

Bahnhof *Uelzen / Deutschland*

Seit Juni 1997 betreiben die Stadtwerke Uelzen auf einer Fläche von 720 m² auf dem Dach des Bahnhofs eine Photovoltaikanlage mit 264 Modulen. Die rahmenlosen Module dienen als wetterfester Dachhautersatz. Die umweltfreundliche Energieproduktion ist ein wichtiger Bestandteil des „Umweltbahnhofs". Der erzeugte Strom wird in das Netz der Stadtwerke eingespeist. Auf der Grundlage des in Uelzen umgesetzten Konzeptes kann die Installation von Photovoltaik-Modulen zu einer Standardvariante bei der Sanierung von Dachflächen der Deutschen Bahn AG werden.

Die Photovoltaikanlagen auf den Bahnsteigdächern wurden bewusst in publikumswirksameren Bereichen installiert, um den Präsentationsnachteil der dachintegrierten Anlage zu kompensieren. Eine Holzstruktur trägt nun im Wechselspiel semitransparente Photovoltaikmodule und Milchglasscheiben, welche die Eternit-Zementplatten der alten Überdachung ersetzen. Es wurden Sondermodule mit einer Größe von 1,00 m x 1,10 m in Überkopfverglasung installiert. Durch einen größeren Abstand der multikristallinen Zellen wurden 20 Prozent Lichtdurchlässigkeit erreicht.

Der Einsatz von semitransparenten Modulen erhöht nicht nur die Aufenthaltsqualität, sondern trägt durch die verlängerte Tageslichtnutzung auch zur Einsparung von Beleuchtungsenergie bei. In der Empfangshalle des Bahnhofsgebäudes kann man sich an einem Terminal über die Funktionsweise und die Leistungsdaten (Stromertrag) der Photovoltaikanlage informieren.

Train Station *Uelzen / Germany*

Since June 1997, the public utility of Uelzen has been operating a photovoltaic facility with 264 modules on a surface of 720 m² on the roof of the station. The frameless modules serve as a substitute for weatherproof roof cladding. Ecologically sound energy production is an important component of the environmentally friendly station. The power generated is fed into the grid of the utility. Based on the model in Uelzen, installation of photovoltaic modules could become standard for the renovation of roof areas of the *Deutsche Bahn AG* (German Railways) buildings.

The additional photovoltaics on the railway platform roofs were deliberately installed in areas that are visible to the public in order to compensate for the lack of visibility of those integrated into the roof. A wooden structure now supports an interplay of semitransparent photovoltaic modules and frosted glass panes that replace the old asbestos cement roofing. Special modules with dimensions of 1.00 m x 1.10 m in overhead glazing have been installed. 20 percent light transmission was achieved by increasing the distance between the multicrystalline cells.

The use of semitransparent modules not only improves the quality of a stop at the station but, through the extended use of daylight, it also helps save energy on lighting. Information about the functioning and performance data (power generation) of the photovoltaic system is available at a terminal in the hall of the station building.

Location:	Uelzen, Germany
Owner:	Deutsche Bahn AG
Architect:	Friedensreich Hundertwasser
Energy consultant:	ISFH
System provider:	Osmer solar
System technology:	SMA
Year:	1997
Energy output:	13.4 kW$_p$
Energy yield:	8 530 kWh/a
Area:	150 m²

Location:	Berlin, Germany
Owner:	Wall AG
Architect:	GK Sekkei
Energy consultant:	Wall AG
System provider:	BEWAG
Year:	2000
Energy output:	141 W_p per module
Energy yield:	100 kWh/a per module
Area:	1.2 m^2

Solare Wartehallen

Berlin / Deutschland; diverse Orte / England

Die in Berlin bereits in 30 Exemplaren stadtweit aufgestellte „Intelligente Wartehalle" fügt sich mit ihrer Transparenz sowohl in das moderne als auch in das historische Stadtbild ein. In das Dach sind monokristalline Standard-Solarzellen der Größe 12,5 cm x 12,5 cm mit Zellabstand 2,5 cm eingebettet. Der erzeugte Strom wird in das öffentliche Netz eingespeist und abends für die integrierten Funktionen wie das e-Info-Terminal, die Fahrgastanzeige und die Beleuchtung der Werbevitrine wieder entnommen. Erweiterungsmöglichkeiten, 20-fach variierbar, sind in allen Größen und Abmessungen möglich. Die Wartehallen können darüber hinaus als Solar-Tankstellen für Elektroroller dienen.

Das *streetsmart*-System für Überdachungen an Haltestellen wurde in England entwickelt. Es ist sehr anpassungsfähig und kann nachträglich in jede Art von Überdachung eingebaut werden. Über 900 *streetsmart*-Systeme wurden bereits in England und anderen europäischen Ländern installiert.
Das System ist multifunktional und kombiniert die Wetterschutzfunktion mit einem energiesparenden Beleuchtungssystem (LEDs) und einer Photovoltaikanlage (monokristalline Photovoltaik-Zellen eingebettet in Polycarbonat) mit nicht sichtbaren langlebigen Batterien. Die Verwendung von Polycarbonat statt Glas macht die Anlagen leicht, flexibel und vandalismussicher. Dadurch, dass die Anlagen nicht an das Stromnetz angeschlossen werden, werden Kosten für Erdarbeiten und Verkabelung sowie Anschluss- und Stromgebühren eingespart.

Solar Shelters
Berlin / Germany; diverse locations / England

In Berlin there are already 30 examples of the transparent "smart bus shelter" that fits in with both the modern and the historical image of the city. Monocrystalline standard solar cells with dimensions of 12.5 cm x 12.5 cm at intervals of 2.5 cm are integrated into the roofs of these shelters. The electricity generated is fed into the public grid and taken from there in the evenings to run the integrated functions such as electronic information terminals, passenger display systems and the lighting of the advertising display cases. Extension options, with 20 possible combinations, are available in all sizes and dimensions. The shelters can also serve as solar service stations for electric scooters.

In England, the "streetsmart" system for shelters has been developed. It is highly adaptable and can be retrofitted into any shelter design. Over 900 systems have already been installed across the United Kingdom and Europe.
The system is multi-functional, combining weather protection with an energy-saving lighting system (LEDs) and photovoltaics (monocrystalline photovoltaic cells integrated in polycarbonate) with non-visible durable batteries. The use of polycarbonate instead of glass makes the system light, flexible and vandalism-proof. Since the facilities are not connected to the grid, costs of excavation work and cabling, as well as connection fees and electricity charges are saved.

Location:	Plymouth etc., England
Architect:	solarcentury
Energy consultant:	solarcentury
System provider:	solarcentury
Year:	2003
Energy output:	280 W_p per module
Energy yield:	200 kWh/a per module
Area:	2.4 m^2

Location:	Bocca di Magra, Italy
Owner:	Comune di Ameglia
Architect:	PVACCEPT / UdK Berlin
Energy consultant:	PVACCEPT / BUSI IMPIANTI
System provider:	PVACCEPT / Würth Solar
Year:	2004
Energy output:	300 W$_p$
Energy yield:	400 kWh/a
Area:	3.6 m^2

Solar-Pergolen *Ameglia – Bocca di Magra / Italien*   PVACCEPT-Demonstrationsanlage

An der Meereseinmündung des Flusses Magra in der Gemeinde Ameglia wurden im Rahmen der Neugestaltung der Uferpromenade am Yachthafen drei solare Pergolen errichtet. Diese bestehen jeweils aus einer schlanken Metallkonstruktion, auf die fünf semitransparente Dünnschichtmodule mit Rundlochmuster in der Spezialgröße 2,40 m x 0,30 m montiert sind. Die Verkabelung wird in den Stahlhohlprofilen der Konstruktion geführt. In den Pergolarahmen ebenso wie in den die Pergolen straßenseitig flankierenden Mauern sind kleine LED-Strahler in den Farben weiß und blau eingebaut, die ihre Energie nachts aus dem von den Modulen tagsüber erzeugten und in Batterien gespeicherten Strom beziehen. Die Batterien und Schaltschränke sind ebenfalls in die neuen Werksteinmauern integriert.

Die drei Pergolen wurden von der Gemeinde in drei unterschiedlichen Blautönen lackiert und fügen sich gut in das maritime Ambiente ein.

Die 2004 errichtete Anlage ist mit einem automatischen System ausgestattet, das Energieerzeugung und -verbrauch misst und von dem die Daten jederzeit zur Kontrolle abgerufen werden können.

Solar Pergolas   *Ameglia – Bocca di Magra / Italy*   PVACCEPT Demonstration Object

In the municipality of Ameglia, at the point where the River Magra flows into the sea, three solar pergolas were erected during reconstruction of the promenade at the yachting harbour. Each of these pergolas consists of a thin metal structure onto which five semitransparent punch-hole thin-film modules (with the special dimensions of 2.40 m x 0.30 m) are mounted. The cabling runs through the hollow steel profiles of the supporting structure. Small LED emitters in white and blue are integrated into the pergola frames and in the walls flanking the pergolas on the side of the road; at night they obtain their power from the electricity which is generated by the modules in the daytime and then stored in batteries. The batteries and switchgear cabinets are also integrated into the new ashlar masonry.

The three pergolas have been painted in three shades of blue by the local communal authority and fit well with the maritime ambience.

The installation, erected in 2004, is equipped with an automatic data logging system that measures power generation and consumption and can be used to call up and check data at any time.

„Sunbrellas" *Hamburg / Deutschland*

Im Mai 2002 wurde ein Entwurfswettbewerb im Fachbereich Architektur der Hochschule für angewandte Wissenschaften (HAW) Hamburg gestartet mit dem Ziel, eine Solarstromanlage zu entwerfen, die zugleich als Schattenspender für die Freiluft-Leseplätze der neuen Bibliothek dienen sollte. Gleichzeitig sollte den Studierenden mit diesem Projekt anhand eines praxisbezogenen Beispiels aktuelles Wissen zu erneuerbaren Energien vermittelt werden, und umweltfreundliche Technik sollte erlebbar gemacht werden. Außerdem sollte so die Sonne selbst (aufgrund der Vergütung des Stromertrags) zur Finanzierung von Studien- und Entwicklungsprojekten im Bereich erneuerbare Energien an der Hochschule beitragen.

Als Sieger gingen die *Sunbrellas* („Sonnenstromschirme") aus diesem Wettbewerb hervor, die durch ihre originelle und attraktive Gestaltung mit einem Spiel aus Licht, Schatten und unerwarteten Durchblicken überzeugten.

Die *Sunbrellas* sind Sonnenschirme mit Tischen und Sitzen, deren Dächer Solargeneratoren tragen. Die jeweils 20 rahmenlosen Solarmodule sind Sonderanfertigungen in der Größe 1,62 m x 0,81 m mit Einscheiben-Sicherheitsglas und einer transparenten Rückseitenfolie und gruppieren sich um eine große Glasscheibe. Sie sind in einen Rahmen eingespannt, der auf zwei durch Speichen verbundenen Ringen ruht. Der äußere Ring hat einen Durchmesser von über sechs Metern und trägt nach außen einen Strahlenkranz. Dieses Dach der tonnenschweren Stahlschirme ist um 20 Grad geneigt und fest nach Süden ausgerichtet. Der erzeugte Strom wird über Wechselrichter in das Netz eingespeist.

Für die Verwirklichung wurde ein Förderverein gegründet. Unterstützt wurde das Projekt durch Spenden und durch das engagierte Entgegenkommen der am Bau beteiligten Firmen; ein Teil der Baukosten wurde außerdem durch Eigenleistungen von Studierenden und Hochschulmitarbeitern eingespart; sogar die Feuerwehr half mit einem Kran bei der Montage. Insgesamt wurden drei Viertel der Kosten durch Spenden und Fördermittel aufgebracht; die restlichen 25 Prozent wurden durch die Hochschule vorfinanziert.

Im September 2003 wurden die fünf „Sonnenstromschirme" auf der Süd-Ost-Terrasse vor der Bibliothek im siebten Stock des neuen Hauptgebäudes der HAW, des sogenannten „blauen Hauses", feierlich in Betrieb genommen und laden jetzt bei schönem Wetter als Sonnenschutz zum Verweilen ein.

Sie belegen auf anschauliche Weise, dass die Hochschule bei der praxisnahen Ausbildung der Studenten ganz bewusst auf umweltschonende Zukunftstechnologien setzt.

Location:	Hamburg, Germany
Owner:	HAW Solar e.V.
Architect:	Hartmut Zehm,
	Jan Kaundinya
Energy consultant:	HAW, Wolfgang Moré
System provider:	Solara AG
Year:	2004
Energy output:	15.5 kW$_p$
Energy yield:	11 950 kWh/a
Area:	130 m^2

"Sunbrellas" *Hamburg / Germany*

In May 2002 a competition was held in the Faculty of Architecture at Hamburg University of Applied Sciences (HAW) with the aim of designing a solar powered system which would also provide shade for seats in the open-air reading room of the new library. At the same time, this project was designed to provide students with up-to-date knowledge of renewable energies by serving as a practical example, and environmentally friendly technology was to be made accessible. Moreover, the sun itself was (through reimbursement for the electricity generated) to thus contribute to the financing of study and development projects in the field of renewable energies at the university.

The "sunbrella" emerged as the winner of this competition, impressive thanks to the original and attractive design with an interplay of light, shade and unexpected transparency.

The "sunbrellas" are sunshades with tables and seats and a roof supporting solar generators. The 20 frameless solar modules of each one, specially manufactured in dimensions of 1.62 m x 0.81 m with tempered safety glass and a transparent backing foil, are grouped around a large pane of glass. They are inserted into a frame supported by two rings connected by spokes. The outside ring has a diameter of over six metres and it supports the 'roof' of the heavy steel umbrella, which is tilted at an angle of 20° and oriented directly to the south. The electricity generated is fed into the grid through power invertors.

An association was founded to implement the project. The latter was financed through donations and through the committed kindness of the companies involved in the construction; construction costs were also saved through

self-help construction work by students and teachers. Even the fire brigade helped with installation by providing a crane. Overall three quarters of the costs were financed through donations and promotion funds; the remaining 25 percent were pre-financed by the university.

In September 2003, the five "sunbrellas" on the south-east terrace in front of the library on the seventh floor of the new main building, known as the "blue building", of the HAW were officially put into operation, and in warm weather they now invite the students to sit and use them as sunshades.

They demonstrate that while giving the students practical training, the university consciously supports new environmentally friendly technology.

Solare Sitzplätze
Rotterdam und Veenendaal / Niederlande

Der solare Sitzplatz wurde mit Blick auf Gemeinden, Firmen und Projektentwickler als Zielgruppen konzipiert, die das innovative und umweltbewusste Image ihrer Institution oder ihres Projekts betonen und öffentlich sichtbar machen wollen. Er kann in öffentlichen Räumen wie auch in Gärten oder Firmenhöfen installiert werden.

Jeder solare Sitzplatz besteht aus einer Metallkonstruktion, die eine runde Überdachung mit integrierten Solarzellen trägt und im Sockelbereich von einer Sitzbank aus Holz umschlossen ist. Der solare Sitzplatz ist vorgefertigt, was den Zeitaufwand für den Aufbau minimiert; lediglich die Glasplatte mit den Solarzellen und eventuelle Lampen müssen vor Ort installiert werden. Die solare Überdachung befindet sich in einer Höhe von 4 m, um das Risiko von Beschädigungen durch Vandalismus zu verringern.

Die Photovoltaikanlage besteht aus einem runden Glas/Glas-Laminat mit einem Durchmesser von 4,20 m, das in vier Segmente unterteilt ist. In jedes dieser Segmente sind quadratische polykristalline blaue Siliziumzellen von 12,5 cm Kantenlänge mit regelmäßigen Zwischenabständen eingebettet. Der erzeugte Strom wird in das Netz eingespeist.

Solar Seats *Rotterdam and Veenendaal / Netherlands*

The solar seat was designed with the following target groups in mind: local authorities, companies and project developers who want to emphasise the innovative and ecologically aware image of their institution or project and make this obvious to the public. It can be installed in public areas as well as in gardens or company courtyards.

Every solar seat consists of a metal construction that supports a round roof with integrated solar cells and is surrounded by a seat made of wood at the base. The solar seat is prefabricated, which minimises the time required for assembly; only the glass pane with the solar cells and any lamps must be installed on site. The solar roof is positioned at a height of 4 m in order to reduce the risk of damage through vandalism.

The photovoltaic system consists of a round glass/glass laminate with a diameter of 4.20 m subdivided into four segments. In each of these segments, square polycrystalline blue silicon cells with edges 12.5 cm long are integrated at regular intervals. The power generated is fed into the grid.

Location:	Rotterdam and Veenendaal, Netherlands
Owner:	Oskomera Solar Power Solutions
Architect:	ENECO Energie
Energy consultant:	Oskomera Solar Power Solutions
System provider:	Oskomera Solar Power Solutions B.V
Year:	2004
Energy output:	540 kW$_p$
Energy yield:	approx. 400 kWh/a
Area:	9 m^2

Multifunktionale Straßenmöbel   *Sant Cugat del Vallés – Barcelona / Spanien*

Die von einem Architekturbüro in Barcelona entwickelten verschiedenen Typen von multifunktionalen Straßenmöbeln, überwiegend Straßenleuchten, sind alle mit kleinen netzgekoppelten Photovoltaikanlagen ausgestattet. Hier werden einige exemplarisch vorgestellt.

Bei der 5 m hohen Straßenleuchte *Bambú* sind die galvanisierten Stahlrohre im oberen Teil schwungvoll gebogen und tragen ein in die Gesamtform integriertes Solarmodul, das so zur Sonne geneigt ist, dass ein maximaler Energieertrag erzielt wird. Bezüglich der Module gibt es Varianten, zum Beispiel mono- oder polykristallin, mit oder ohne Aluminiumrahmen. Die Größe ist auf ca. 1,30 m x 0,70 m festgelegt.

Dies gilt auch für die Modelle *Curva* und *Cuore*, in deren elegant und ungebrochen geschwungene Formen zusätzlich eine Sitzbank integriert ist, die Platz für zwei Personen bietet. Diese solaren Sitzbänke kombinieren sensible Ästhetik mit effizienter Stromerzeugung und sind bestens für den öffentlichen Raum, für Parks und Gärten geeignet.

Die autonomen Objekte sind in der Lage, den Strom für acht Stunden durchgängiger Beleuchtung bei 100 Prozent Leistung zu liefern. Im Winter, wenn die Sonneneinstrahlung reduziert ist und weniger Strom produziert wird, kann die Lichtleistung der Lampen auf 50 Prozent heruntergeregelt werden, um den Verbrauch zu reduzieren.

Architect:	siarq
	(Studio Itinerante Arquitectura)
Energy consultant:	siarq
System provider:	Isofotón
Energy output:	110 W_p
Energy yield:	150 kWh/a
Area:	0.91 m²

Multi-functional Street Furniture   *Sant Cugat del Vallés – Barcelona / Spain*

The different types of multi-functional street furniture developed by an architect's office in Barcelona, mainly streetlights, are all equipped with small grid-connected photovoltaic systems. A few examples of these are presented here.

The galvanised steel tubes of the 5 m high streetlight *Bambú* are elegantly curved at the top and support a solar module which is integrated into the overall form and tilted towards the sun at an angle so as to maximise power generation. Different versions of modules are used, e.g. monocrystalline or polycrystalline, with or without an aluminium frame. The size is at approximately 1.30 m x 0.70 m.

This also applies to the models *Curva* and *Cuore* which have a bench to seat two people integrated into their elegantly and continuously curved forms. These solar benches combine sensitive aesthetics with efficient power generation and are best suited to public areas, parks and gardens.

The autonomous objects are capable of providing enough power for eight hours of constant lighting at full capacity. In winter, when solar radiation is reduced and less electricity is produced, the luminous power of the lights can be regulated to 50 percent in order to reduce consumption.

Selbstleuchtende „Solarflaggen"
Porto Venere / Italien
PVACCEPT-Demonstrationsanlage

Im Innenhof der denkmalgeschützten Festungsanlage *Castello Doria* in Porto Venere wurden in sechs Mauerbögen jeweils drei sogenannte *solar flags* („Solarflaggen") an Stahlseilen hängend montiert. Die Eingriffe in das historische Gemäuer für die Befestigung der Seile wurden unter anderem dadurch gering gehalten, dass vorhandene Öffnungen genutzt wurden.

Bei den Modulen handelt es sich um transparente, leicht gekrümmte Elemente aus Acrylglas, in die semitransparente graue Solarzellen eingebettet sind. Sie sind aufgrund von integrierten LEDs selbstleuchtend.

Der von den 18 *solar flags* erzeugte Strom wird in einer Batterie gespeichert und nachts zur eigenen Beleuchtung der Module verwendet.

Die *solar flags* können auch unterschiedliche Farben haben – sowohl die Module selbst wie auch die integrierte Beleuchtung. Ihre Anwendungsmöglichkeiten sind äußerst vielfältig. Da sie in beliebiger Anzahl aneinandergereiht und auf unterschiedliche Arten und Unterkonstruktionen montiert werden können, sind sie zur – auch temporären – Platzgestaltung genauso geeignet wie beispielsweise zur Gestaltung von „Solarbäumen" oder „Leuchtbaldachinen".

Die 2004 errichtete Anlage ist mit einem automatischen System ausgestattet, das Energieerzeugung und -verbrauch misst und von dem die Daten jederzeit zur Kontrolle abgerufen werden können.

Location:	Porto Venere, Italy
Owner:	State of Italy; administration:
	Soprintendenza per i beni
	architettonici e per
	il paesaggio della Liguria
Architect:	PVACCEPT / UdK Berlin
Energy consultant:	PVACCEPT / BUSI IMPIANTI
System provider:	PVACCEPT / Sunways
	Photovoltaics Technology
Year:	2004
Energy output:	225 W_p
Energy yield:	180 kWh/a
Area:	4.4 m^2

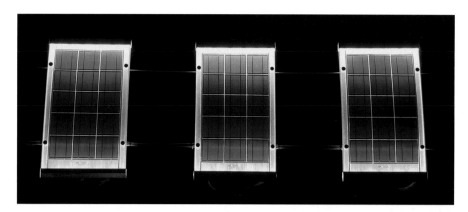

Luminous "Solar Flags" *Porto Venere / Italy* PVACCEPT Demonstration Object

In the inner courtyard of the listed monument *Castello Doria* in Porto Venere, three "solar flags" have been mounted, hanging on steel wires, in each of six wall arches. Intervention to the historic walls was minimised by using existing openings to fix the wires.

The modules are transparent, slightly curved acrylic glass components with embedded semitransparent grey solar cells. They are luminous because of integrated light emitting diodes (LEDs).

The power generated by the 18 "solar flags" is stored in a battery and used to light up the modules at night.

Both the modules themselves and the integrated lighting may also be produced in different colours. The possible applications of the "solar flags" are extremely varied. Since any number of them can be added and mounted in various ways and on various sub-structures, they are just as suited for the – also temporary – design of public squares as for the use in "solar trees" or "luminous canopies".

The installation, erected in 2004, is equipped with an automatic data logging system that measures power generation and consumption and can be used to call up and check data at any time.

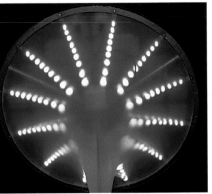

Architect:	Christoph Behling
Energy consultant:	Kopf Solardesign
System provider:	Kopf Solardesign
Year:	2000
Solar Fountain	
Energy output:	55; 110 W_p
Energy yield:	42; 84 kWh/a
Area:	0.36; 0.72 m^2
Solar Grass	
Energy output:	55 W_p
Energy yield:	42 kWh/a
Area:	0.36 m^2

Solarbrunnen und „Solargräser" *diverse Orte / Deutschland*

Diese Objekte stehen hier stellvertretend für die zahlreichen Möglichkeiten, Photovoltaik bei der künstlerischen Gestaltung im öffentlichen Raum einzubeziehen.

Der Solarbrunnen wurde als Gestaltungselement für größere Wasserflächen entwickelt. Es handelt sich um speziell angefertigte Glas/Folie-Sondermodule mit einer weißen Folie. Bislang wurden kristalline Zellen im Format 10 cm x 10 cm verwendet, in Zukunft werden es Zellen im Format 15 cm x 15 cm sein. Durch einen speziellen Schwimmkörper wird erreicht, dass der Solarbrunnen wenige Zentimeter über der Wasseroberfläche „schwebt"; er wird über Gewichte im Gewässergrund verankert. Seine Pumpe wird direkt über das Solarmodul mit Energie versorgt.

Je nach Sonneneinstrahlung wird die Fontäne höher, erreicht bei bester Einstrahlung ihr Maximum und versiegt bei Dunkelheit. Wenn es sich um eine größere Installation mit mehreren Einzelbrunnen handelt, können diese mit einer zentralen Batterie ausgestattet werden, um sie auch abends noch in Betrieb zu halten. Dann ist auch eine Beleuchtung der Wasserfontänen, zum Beispiel in wechselnden Farben, möglich.

Die „Solargräser" sind ebenfalls Installationen für den Außenbereich. Ihre auf höchste dynamische Belastungen ausgelegten 9 m hohen „Stängel" bestehen aus speziellem nichtrostendem Edelstahl und sind ca. 2 m tief im Boden verankert. Die transluzenten „Blüten" haben einen Durchmesser von ca. 1 m.

Bei Einsetzen der Dämmerung geben die „Gräser" die tagsüber in einer Batterie gesammelte Energie wieder ab. Gespeist wird die Batterie durch ein im „Blütenkelch" angeordnetes rundes, speziell angefertigtes Glas/Folie-Solarmodul mit kristallinen Zellen. Batterie und Laderegler befinden sich in einem Bodeneinbaugehäuse. Die Beleuchtung der „Blüte" erfolgt über mehr als hundert ultrahelle weiße Leuchtdioden (LED) von insgesamt 12 W Leistung. Die Leuchtdauer beträgt ohne Sonne vier Tage bei ca. 6 bis 8 Betriebsstunden pro Nacht (Steuerung über Dämmerungssensor und Zeitschaltuhr).

Solar Fountain and "Solar Grasses"
diverse locations / Germany

These installations are just some examples of the numerous ways photovoltaics may be part of an artistic design in public areas.

The solar fountain was developed as an architectural feature for larger expanses of water. It is based on specially manufactured glass/foil modules with white foil. Crystalline cells measuring 10 cm x 10 cm have been used to date and cells measuring 15 cm x 15 cm will be used in the future.

A special float makes it possible for the solar fountain to be positioned a few centimetres above the surface of the water; it is anchored using weights. Its pump is supplied with energy directly from the solar module.

The jet of the fountain becomes higher depending on the level of solar radiation, it reaches its maximum when radiation is highest and abates when night falls. If the installation comprises several individual fountains, these can be equipped with a central battery in order to keep them operating in the evenings as well. Then it is, for example, also possible to illuminate the water jets in alternating colours.

The "solar grasses" are also installations for outdoors. Their 9 m high "stems" are made of special high-grade stainless steel designed to withstand high dynamic pressure and anchored into the ground approximately 2 m deep. The translucent "flowers" have a diameter of approximately 1 m.

When dusk begins to fall, the "grasses" release the energy accumulated in a battery during the day. The battery is fed through a round custom–made glass/foil solar module with crystalline cells arranged in the "calyx". The battery and charge regulator are located in casing on the ground. The "flower" is lit using more than a hundred ultra-bright white light emitting diodes (LEDs) with a total output of 12 W. Without sun the lighting operates for four nights approximately 6-8 hours each (controlled by a twilight sensor and a time switch).

Industriegebäude an der Autobahn
Duisburg / Deutschland

Aufgrund seiner exponierten Lage an der A 42 in der Nähe von Duisburg wurde bei der Fassadensanierung des Produktionsgebäudes aus den 1970er Jahren besonderer Wert darauf gelegt, zu demonstrieren, dass Industriebauten nicht zwangsläufig mit Tristesse und Kühle gleichzusetzen sind. Während die Form der Wetterschutzfassaden von den Architekten gestaltet wurde, übernahm ein Designbüro das Farbkonzept. Dabei war die Integration einer Photovoltaikanlage von Anfang an geplant.

Damit sich das Gebäude harmonisch in die umgebende Landschaft integriert, wurden auf einer Fassadenfläche von ca. 1400 m² in aufeinander abgestimmten Grüntönen die Photovoltaikelemente im Wechsel mit Blech in wellenförmigen Streifen angebracht. Insgesamt 1004 Solarmodule wurden auf sechs nach Süden ausgerichteten und bis zu 24 m hohen Fassadenfeldern angeordnet. Die Solarelemente wurden im Abstand von 33 cm seitlich an der vorhandenen Stahl-Unterkonstruktion mit Hilfe zusätzlicher Profile und Edelstahlschrauben befestigt und überlappen in der Senkrechten mit jeweils 10 cm.

Die Module bestehen aus amorphen siliziumlegierten Dünnschichten, die auf ein Trägermaterial aus Edelstahl auflaminiert sind. Vier verschiedene Modulgrößen kamen zur Anwendung: 0,29 m x 2,54 m; 0, 48 m x 1,50 m; 0,48 m x 2,81 m und 0,48 m x 5,57 m. Die Anlage ist netzgekoppelt.

Dieses Beispiel steht hier gleichermaßen für Fassadensanierung und für die optisch Integration eines Gebäudes in die umgebende Landschaft unter Nutzung einer Photovoltaikanlage als gestalterisches Element.

Industrial Plant at Motorway   *Duisburg / Germany*

Owing to the prominent location of this 1970s production building on the A 42 by Duisburg, the particular intention within the course of the façade renovation was to demonstrate that industrial buildings don't necessarily have to be cold, bleak and sterile. While architects were responsible for the formal design of the weather protection façade, a design studio was contracted for the colour design. The inclusion of a photovoltaic system was planned from the very outset.

To ensure that the building blends harmoniously into the surrounding landscape, alternate photovoltaic elements and metal panels in co-ordinating shades of green were added to the façade in a wave-like design, covering a total area of around 1,400 m². A total of 1,004 solar modules were mounted onto six south-facing façade sections that are up to 24 metres high. At a distance of 33 cm, the solar elements were mounted laterally, with a 10 cm vertical overlap, onto the existing steel support frame using additional profiles and stainless steel bolts .

The modules consist of wafer-thin layers of amorphous silicon, laminated onto a base layer of stainless steel. Four different module sizes were used: 0.29 m x 2.54 m; 0.48 m x 1.50 m; 0.48 m x 2.81 m and 0.48 m x 5.57 m. The photovoltaic system is grid-connected.

This plant is an example of both building façade renovation and the visual integration of a building into the surrounding landscape using a photovoltaic system as a design feature.

Location:	Duisburg, Germany
Owner:	ThyssenKrupp Stahl
Architect:	Czerny - Gunia
Energy consultant:	ThyssenKrupp Solartec
System provider:	ThyssenKrupp Solartec
Year:	2002
Energy output:	51.06 kW$_p$
Energy yield:	32 130 kWh/a
Area:	1 000 m²

Überdachung einer Aussichtsterrasse *Remseck / Deutschland*

Zentraler Punkt der neuen Straßen- und Ufergestaltung in Remseck im Bereich zwischen der Dorfstraße und der Straße „Am Remsufer" ist eine mit einer schwungvollen Photovoltaikanlage überdachte Aussichtsterrasse. Mit der Photovoltaikanlage wollten die Planer nicht nur demonstrativ eine umweltfreundliche Form der Stromgewinnung aufgreifen, sondern zugleich ein städtebaulich interessantes Objekt schaffen, das neugierige Blicke anziehen soll.

Auf eine Stahlkonstruktion wurden insgesamt 100 CIS-Dünnschicht-Module in der Standardgröße 0,60 m x 1,20 m – als Sonderausführung in Überkopfverglasung – montiert. Sie sind semitransparent: Zellstreifen und transparente Streifen wechseln sich ab; der Grad der Transparenz liegt bei ca. 20 Prozent ihrer Fläche. Die netzgekoppelte Photovoltaikanlage produziert rein rechnerisch den Strom für die Beleuchtung der zwei neu gestalteten Straßen.

Um zu verdeutlichen, wie Photovoltaik funktioniert, wurde eine digitale Messtafel installiert, welche die momentane Stromgewinnung, den bisher erzeugten Strom seit Inbetriebnahme sowie die bisherige Einsparung an umweltschädlichen Emissionen (CO_2) aufzeigt.

Location:	Remseck / Neckar, Germany
Owner:	Stadt Remseck am Neckar
Architect:	Dipl.-Ing. Peter Blumhagen, Planungsamt Remseck
Energy Consultant:	Würth Solergy
System Provider:	Würth Solar
Year:	2003
Energy Output:	4.6 kW$_p$
Energy yield:	4 000 kWh/a
Area:	72 m²

Panoramic Terrace Roof *Remseck / Germany*

The central point of the reconstructed street and embankment in Remseck, in the area between *Dorfstraße* and the street *Am Remsufer*, is a panoramic terrace covered with an elegantly curved photovoltaic roof. The planners' intention was to design an environmentally friendly form of power generation; at the same time the installation should contribute to the urban development of Remseck and attract inquisitive glances from passers-by.

A total of 100 CIS thin-film modules, in a standard size of 0.60 m x 1.20 m, were mounted on a steel structure and as a special model with overhead glazing. The modules are semitransparent, i.e. solar cell strips are alternated with transparent strips. The degree of transparency is approximately 20 percent of the surface. The grid-connected photovoltaic system effectively produces enough electricity to light the two reconstructed streets.

In order to demonstrate how photovoltaics work, a digital instrument panel has been installed. This displays the present level of power generation, the total power generated since operation began and the reduction in harmful emissions (CO_2) up to date.

Bei den Carports in Emmerthal handelt es sich um eine experimentelle Demonstrationsanlage. Sie wurde am Südhang des Ohrbergs errichtet, auf dem Gelände des 1993 gebauten Instituts für Solarenergieforschung, das sich unter anderem mit Photovoltaik beschäftigt. Es sollte damit eine gebäudeunabhängige Solaranlage mit gleichzeitiger Schutzdachfunktion als innovative Demonstration praxisbezogener Photovoltaiknutzung präsentiert werden. Gleichzeitig kann die Anlage die Funktion einer Solartankstelle für Elektrofahrzeuge erfüllen, denn die stellplatzbezogene Fläche liefert pro Jahr Energie für ca. 10.000 km Fahrleistung. Eine solche Stromtankstelle wurde unter einem Doppelcarport aufgestellt und wird vom Bundesverband Solare Mobilität (Solarmobil) betrieben.

Die Konstruktion ist als Einzelcarport, Doppelcarport oder Reihenanlage möglich. Es handelt sich dabei um einen Photovoltaikschirm (16 Module pro Einzelcarport), der jeweils für einen einzelnen oder doppelten Stellplatz von einer einzigen Stütze mit gespreizten Streben gehalten wird. Jede beliebige Anzahl von Parkplätzen kann damit stützenfrei überdacht werden. Bei gleicher Dachneigung von 15 Grad wird zwischen zwei Typen (Einfahrt von Norden bzw. Süden) unterschieden.

Unterschiedliche Module mit einem hohem Wirkungsgrad und der Eignung für Überkopfverglasung kamen zur Anwendung: monokristalline beidseitig lichtempfindliche (Größe: 1,32 m x 0,66 m), semitransparente Glas/Glas-Module mit einer Modultransparenz von 41 Prozent, polykristalline mit einer Leistung von 38,4 W_p und monokristalline mit einer Leistung von 50 W_p; einige davon stammten von einer früheren Solartankstelle, die auf dem Gelände der Expo 2000 in Hannover gestanden hatte.

Entsprechend den unterschiedlichen Modultypen wurden Teilgeneratoren installiert, die über Wechselrichter in das öffentliche Stromnetz einspeisen.

Bei dem Carport in Potenza sind die Photovoltaikflächen in Reihen zu je drei Modulen aus monokristallinen Zellen auf eine Stahlkonstruktion montiert, die als „Faradayscher Käfig" gleichzeitig die elektronische Ausstattung so gut wie möglich gegen Blitzschlag schützen soll. Die Module haben die Abmessungen 0,99 m x 1,66 m. Die Anlage ist auf leichtes Austauschen bzw. Entfernen der Module im Zuge von Instandhaltungsmaßnahmen und auf Erweiterung der elektrischen Kapazität ausgelegt. Sie wurde von einem Privateigentümer errichtet, um Energiekosten zu sparen und die Photovoltaik generell zu fördern.

Location:	Emmerthal, Germany
Owner:	Institut für Solarenergieforschung
Architect:	Poos Isensee
Energy consultant:	Institut für Solarforschung
System provider:	Elektroma, Solarnova
Year:	2000
Energy output:	12.9 kW_p
Energy yield:	9 418 kWh/a
Area:	154 m²

Location:	Basilicata, Italy
Owner:	Private
Energy consultant:	Aci Service Engineering s.r.l.
System provider:	IBC SOLAR
System technology:	Aci Service s.r.l.
Year:	2004
Energy output:	5.7 kW$_p$
Energy yield:	7 200 kWh/a
Area:	42 m^2

Carports *Emmerthal / Germany; Potenza / Italy*

The carports in Emmerthal are an experimental demonstration system, which was installed on the premises of the Institute for Solar Energy Research. The latter was built in 1993 on the south side of the *Ohrberg* in Emmerthal and carries out research, among other things, in the field of photovoltaics. The intention was to develop a stand-alone solar system that doubles as a car shed in order to demonstrate how photovoltaic systems can be used innovatively in everyday applications. At the same time, the system can function as a solar recharging station for electric vehicles, with the "park and charge" area providing enough energy for around 10,000 km of mileage per year. A recharging station of this kind was built beneath a double carport and is run by the German Association of Solar Mobility (*Solarmobil*).

In terms of design, single, double or multi-space carports are possible. The basic structure is a photovoltaic umbrella (16 modules per single carport) which is supported by one single support column with spoke-like projections at the top for one single or double parking space. In this way, any given number of parking spaces can be covered without disturbing pillars. Two different types exist (entrance from the north or from the south), but in both cases the roof is tilted at an angle of 15°.

Different types of high-efficiency modules which are suitable for use as overhead glazing were employed: monocrystalline, double-sided photosensitive (dimensions: 1.32 m x 0.66 m) semitransparent glass/glass modules with 41 percent module transparency, polycrystalline with 38.4 W$_p$ output power and monocrystalline with 50 W$_p$ output power; some of these originated from a former solar recharging station which had been located in the Hannover fair area. In accordance with the different module types, generator installations were used to feed the electricity into the local power grid via inverters.

The carport in Potenza features photovoltaic panels mounted onto a steel structure in rows of three modules comprising monocrystalline solar cells. This steel structure functions as a Faraday cage whose purpose is to protect the electrical equipment from lightning. The modules measure 0.99 m x 1.66 m.

The design of the facility allows easy removal or replacement of the modules in order for maintenance work to be carried out and for the extension of the electrical capacity. This system was installed by a private property owner in order to save on energy costs and promote the use of photovoltaic systems in general.

Kombinierte Schallschutzwand *Freising / Deutschland*

Hier wurden Photovoltaikanlage und Schall-schutzwand zu einem „intelligenten" System kombiniert. Auf einer Länge von über 900 m und einer Fläche von rund 4000 m² kamen unterschiedliche Photovoltaikmodule zum Einsatz: Im Sockelbereich wurden konventionelle monokristalline Module einer Größe von jeweils 1,31 m x 0,97 m installiert, während der für den Schallschutz relevante Bereich mit speziell angefertigten innovativen Modulen bestückt wurde. Bei letzteren handelt es sich um Pilotmodule aus einem von der Europäischen Kommission geförderten Projekt, bei denen die Photovoltaik auf einen keramischen Träger laminiert wurde.

Aufgrund ihrer keramischen Träger sind bei dem realisierten Konzept die innovativen Photovoltaikelemente selbst schallschluckend. Dies unterscheidet die Anlage von den sonst üblichen Konstruktionen, bei denen Photovoltaikmodule auf separate Schallschutzwände montiert werden. Um Unterschiede in der Stromerzeugung feststellen zu können, werden die Werte der beiden unterschiedlichen Systeme getrennt gemessen. Die gewonnene elektrische Energie wird abschnittsweise mit zentralen Wechselrichtern von Gleichstrom in Wechselstrom umgeformt und über eine neu errichtete Trafostation in das Netz eingespeist.

Location:	Freising, Germany
Owner:	Stadtwerke Freising
Energy consultant:	WIP
	Gehrlicher
System provider:	Isofotón
Year:	2003
Energy output:	500 kW$_p$
Energy yield:	460 000 kWh/a
Area:	4 000 m^2

Combined Noise Protection Wall *Freising / Germany*

In this project, a photovoltaic system and noise protection wall were combined to form an "intelligent" system. Different types of photovoltaic modules were used across a length of more than 900 m and an area of around 4000 m^2: in the base area conventional monocrystalline modules measuring 1.31 m x 0.97 m were installed, while for the relevant sound-proof area an innovative module type made especially for this purpose was used. The modules are pilot products which were developed in a project funded by the European Commission and comprise photovoltaic elements laminated onto a ceramic base. What is innovative about these modules is the fact that the photovoltaic elements themselves are noise-protecting due to the ceramic base, setting this type of photovoltaic system apart from conventional designs where the photovoltaic modules are mounted onto separate sound-proof panels.

To determine the difference in terms of power generation, the outputs of the two types of systems are measured separately. At given intervals, the electrical energy gained is converted from direct to alternating current using central inverters and fed into the power grid via a recently installed transformer station.

Großflächiger Photovoltaikpark Höslwang / Deutschland

Höslwang in Bayern, der Standort der Anlage, gehört mit einer Globalstrahlung von 1148 kWh/m^2 zu den idealen Standorten für Sonnenenergienutzung in Deutschland. Die für die Anlage benötigte Grundstücksfläche von ca. sechs Hektar wurde durch die Bauherrin, die BGZ Beteiligungsgesellschaft Zukunftsenergien AG, von einem Landwirt gepachtet, der sie auch weiterhin zur Ziegenbeweidung nutzt. Die Kommanditisten der Betreibergesellschaft stellen mit ihren Einlagen das Eigenkapital der Gesellschaft. Die jährlichen Überschüsse werden an die Kommanditisten ausgeschüttet, was die Rückzahlung des eingebrachten Kapitals zuzüglich einer „Verzinsung" bedeutet.

Das Grundstück ist an drei Seiten von Wald umsäumt. Um entsprechende Verschattung zu vermeiden, wurde die Solaranlage mit ausreichendem Abstand zu den Bäumen installiert. Der Verpächter, der in der Nachbarschaft wohnt, sorgt für die Sicherheit der Anlage vor mutwilliger Beschädigung.
Im Rahmen des ökologischen Gesamtkonzeptes und mit dem Ziel höchstmöglicher Umweltverträglichkeit, minimaler Veränderung des Landschaftsbildes und geringen Flächenverbrauchs wurde die Fläche nicht eingeebnet und versiegelt; stattdessen werden die Module von einer Konstruktion aus Robinienholz mit Pfahlgründung, also ohne Betonfundament,

getragen, die dem sanften Schwung der Landschaft folgt.
Die Module bestehen jeweils aus 72 (6 x 12) in Serie geschalteten 12,5 cm x 12,5 cm großen monokristallinen Siliziumzellen. Sie wurden in vier Reihen à jeweils 18 Modulen übereinander pro Einheit auf die Untergestelle montiert. In die Gestelle integriert wurden die Halterungen für die Generatoranschluss- und die Koppelkästen sowie das Blitzschutzsystem. Die Anlage ist netzgekoppelt.

Location:	Höslwang, Germany
Owner:	BGZ Beteiligungsgesellschaft Zukunftsenergien AG
Energy consultant:	Shell Solar
System provider:	Shell Solar
Year:	2004
Energy output:	1.8 MW$_p$
Energy yield:	1 830 000 kWh/a
Area:	13 365 m^2

Large-Scale Photovoltaic Park *Höslwang / Germany*

Being one of the sunniest regions in Germany, Höslwang in Bavaria, where the photovoltaic park is situated, is an ideal location for the generation of solar energy within Germany, boasting a solar irradiation of 1,148 kWh/m^2.

The owner, *Beteiligungsgesellschaft Zukunfts-energien AG* (BGZ), leases the land required for the installation – approximately 6 hectares – from a farmer who continues to use it as pasture fields for his goats. The company's equity capital comes from its limited partners. The annual excess is distributed to the limited partners, which basically amounts to the repayment of the capital contribution plus "interest".

The land is surrounded by forest on three sides. To prevent the solar system from being shaded by the trees, it was installed at sufficient distance from the surrounding forest. The lessor, who lives in the neighbouring area, is responsible for ensuring that no wilful damage is caused to the photovoltaic park.

In keeping with the overall ecological concept and with the objectives of achieving a maximum degree of environmental compatibility, minimum change to the surrounding natural environment and minimum land use, the area was not levelled off and sealed; instead, the modules are mounted onto a timber-framed struc-

ture using Robinia wood on a pile foundation (i.e. concrete foundations were not used). In its design, the wooden structure concurs with the soft contours of the surrounding landscape.

Each module comprises 72 (6 x 12) monocrystalline silicon solar cells connected in series; each cell is 12.5 cm x 12.5 cm in size. The modules are mounted onto support frames in units comprising four rows of 18 modules each. The generator terminal box and the connector box, as well as a lightning protection system are also integrated into the support frames. The photovoltaic system is grid-connected.

Location:	L'Hospitalet de Llobregat / Barcelona
Owner:	Municipality of L'Hospitalet de Llobregat
Architect:	siarq (Studio Itinerante Arquitectura)
Energy consultant:	siarq, Solaring
System provider:	Isofotón
Year:	2002
Energy output:	2.5 kW$_p$
Energy yield:	3 800 kWh/a
Area:	25 m^2

Skulptur *Dinosaurio*   *L'Hospitalet de Llobregat – Barcelona / Spanien*

Der von einem Architekturbüro in Barcelona entwickelte „Dinosaurier" ist eine hocheffiziente Solaranlage und Leuchte und kann als zusätzlich Schatten spendende Skulptur sowohl im Stadtraum wie auch in der Landschaft einen Platz finden. Der „Dinosaurier" ist maximal 13 m hoch und trägt zwei integrierte Flutlichtlampen von 250 bzw. 400 W sowie 18 kristalline Photovoltaikmodule im Format von ca. 1,31 m x 0,70 m und mit einer Gesamtfläche von 25 m^2. Die 35-Grad-Neigung der Module garantiert optimale Sonneneinstrahlung. Die geschwun-gene Tragstruktur erweckt den Eindruck dynamischer Bewegung, und die chromatischen Charakteristika der verwendeten Materialien Corten-Stahl (rostfarben) und Solarmodule (High-Tech-Blau) bilden eine harmonische Kombination.

Die gezeigte Anlage steht in L'Hospitalet de Llobregat; der erzeugte Strom wird gegen Vergütung in das lokale Stromnetz eingespeist. Der Jahresgesamtertrag eines „Dinosauriers" beträgt bis zu 3800 kWh.

Dinosaurio **Sculpture**   *L'Hospitalet de Llobregat – Barcelona / Spain*

The "dinosaur", which was developed by a studio of architecture in Barcelona, is a high-efficiency solar and lighting system which can also be used as a sculpture and provide shade in both city and rural areas. The "dinosaur" measures a maximum of 13 m in height and has two integrated floodlights of 250 or 400 W, plus 18 crystalline photovoltaic modules measuring approximately 1.31 m x 0.70 m each and covering a total area of 25 m². The modules are tilted at an angle of 35° for optimum sun exposure. The curved support structure creates the impression of dynamic movement and the chromatic characteristics of the Corten steel structure blend harmoniously with the high-tech blue of the modules.

The system shown is located in L'Hospitalet de Llobregat; the power generated is fed into the local power grid against reimbursement. The electricity production of one "dinosaur" can reach 3,800 kWh per year.

Technische Grundlagen   Technical Basics

Sonnenenergie

Die Strahlung der Sonne besteht aus elektromagnetischen Wellen mit einer breiten spektralen Verteilung. Die höchste Strahlungsintensität und mit ca. 50 Prozent der Hauptteil der Energie liegt im Bereich des sichtbaren Lichts mit Wellenlängen von 380 bis 780 nm (Nanometern) (blau-rot). Dazu kommen Infrarot- und UV-Strahlung, die für das menschliche Auge nicht sichtbar sind. Im Rahmen der Photovoltaik ist eine Betrachtung im Quantenbild sinnvoll: Danach besteht Licht aus Quanten unterschiedlicher Energie, auch **Photonen** genannt.

Die eingestrahlte und nicht von Staub, Wolken und Ozon absorbierte Energiemenge wird als **Globalstrahlung** bezeichnet und trifft auf der Erde in Form von direkter und diffuser (reflektierter) Sonneneinstrahlung auf. Die Energie der Einstrahlung wird allerdings vom Grad der Bewölkung, von der Höhenlage des jeweiligen Ortes und dem Sonnenstand (Jahreszeit, Tageszeit, geographische Breite) beeinflusst und ist nur am Äquator relativ konstant.

An einem klaren Tag strahlt die Sonne maximal eine Leistung von 1 kW (Kilowatt) auf eine rechtwinklig zur Sonne orientierte Fläche von 1 m². In Nordeuropa summiert sich diese Leistung pro Jahr auf durchschnittlich ca. 800 bis 1000 kWh (Kilowatt-Stunden); in Südeuropa liegt dieser Durchschnittswert höher, nämlich bei 1300 bis 1500 kWh pro Jahr.

Solartechnologie

Die Solartechnologie macht sich die Sonnenenergie zunutze. Es gibt dabei zwei unterschiedliche Arten von sogenannten Generatoren: **thermische** und **photovoltaische**. Sie unterscheiden sich nicht nur in ihrer Funktionsweise, sondern auch in ihrem Erscheinungsbild. Ein thermischer Generator – ein **Kollektor** – verwandelt die Strahlung der Sonne in Wärmeenergie; die Wärme wird in Wasser gespeichert und transportiert und für Heizzwecke oder Warmwasserbereitung genutzt. Ein photovoltaischer Generator – ein **Solarmodul** – verwandelt die Strahlungsenergie des Sonnenlichts direkt in elektrische Energie.

Photovoltaischer Effekt

Der Begriff Photovoltaik leitet sich vom griechischen Wort für Licht (phos) und der Einheit der elektrischen Spannung (Volt) ab. Der **photovoltaische** Effekt bezeichnet die Freisetzung und räumliche Trennung von positiven und negativen Ladungsträgern in einem Festkörper (**Halbleiter**).

Bei Halbleitern können durch das Einbringen von unterschiedlichen Fremdatomen (**Dotieren**) negativ geladene Elektronen („n-Dotierung") oder die positiv geladenen Gegenspieler, sogenannte Defektelektronen oder „Löcher" („p-Dotierung") freigesetzt werden. Eine Verbindung zwischen einem p- und einem n-Leiter stellt einen sogenannten p-n-Übergang dar. In ihm besteht ein elektrisches Feld. Wird der p-n-Übergang mit Lichtenergie bestrahlt, werden durch Lichtabsorption weitere Ladungsträger erzeugt, die durch das elektrische Feld bewegt werden. Es entsteht ein elektrischer Strom, der so lange fließt, wie das Licht scheint. Wird dieser Strom nicht abgeleitet, entsteht eine elektrische Spannung zwischen n- und p-Bereich.

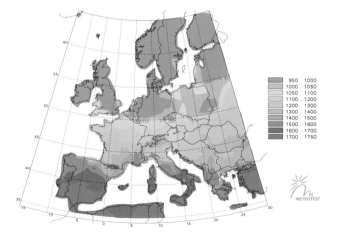

Durchschnittliche Globalstrahlung in Europa in kWh/a
Average global radiation in Europe in kWh/a

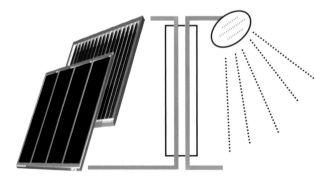

Solarthermischer Generator
Solar thermal generator

Solar Energy

Solar radiation consists of electromagnetic waves of a broad spectral distribution. The largest part with approx. 50 percent comprises visible radiation of wavelengths between 380 and 789 nm (nanometres) (blue-red).The remaining part consists of infrared radiation and ultraviolet radiation which are not visible for human eyes. For an understanding of photovoltaics, a consideration of the quantum picture is appropriate: According to this, light consists of quanta of different energies, also called **photons**.

The incident part of the energy, which is not absorbed by dust, clouds and ozone, is called **global radiation**. It consists of direct and diffuse (reflected) radiation. The incident energy depends on the degree of cloudiness, the altitude of the location and the position of the sun mainly depending on season, daytime and geographic latitude. Only at the equator it is relatively constant.

On a clear day the sun radiates a maximum of 1 kW (kilowatt) onto a rectangular area of 1 m^2 oriented perpendicular to the incoming radiation. In northern Europe this power adds on average to an annual energy of 800 to 1000 kWh (kilowatt hours), in southern Europe this value is higher, namely about 1300 to 1500 kWh per year.

Solar Technology

Solar technology exploits solar energy. There are two distinct kinds of so-called generators: **thermal** and **photovoltaic** ones. They differ not only in the principle of operation but also in their appearance. A solar thermal generator – a **collector** – converts solar radiation into thermal energy, which is stored and transported by water or other liquids and is used for room heating or provision of hot water. A photovoltaic generator – a **solar module** – converts the radiation energy of the sun directly into electric energy.

The Photovoltaic Effect

The term photovoltaic is derived from the Greek word for light (phos) and the unit of electric voltage (volt). The **photovoltaic effect** takes place by light-induced generation and spatial separation of positively and negatively charged carriers in a solid (**semiconductor**).

In semiconductors negatively charged electrons or their positively charged counterparts (so-called defect electrons or "holes") can be liberated by introducing different foreign atoms (**doping**) into the lattice ("n-doping", respectively "p-doping"). A contact between a p-doped and an n-doped semiconductor is called a p-n junction. This region maintains an electric field. If it is irradiated by light, photons are absorbed and generate additional free charge carriers, which are moved by the built-in electric field. Thus an electric current is created, which will flow as long as the light is shining. If the current is not conducted away, a voltage between the p- and n-regions is generated.

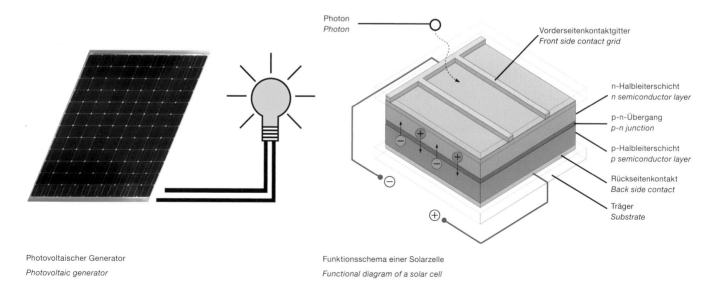

Photovoltaischer Generator
Photovoltaic generator

Funktionsschema einer Solarzelle
Functional diagram of a solar cell

Photon
Photon

Vorderseitenkontaktgitter
Front side contact grid

n-Halbleiterschicht
n semiconductor layer

p-n-Übergang
p-n junction

p-Halbleiterschicht
p semiconductor layer

Rückseitenkontakt
Back side contact

Träger
Substrate

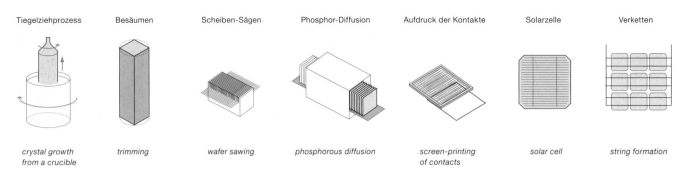

| Tiegelziehprozess | Besäumen | Scheiben-Sägen | Phosphor-Diffusion | Aufdruck der Kontakte | Solarzelle | Verketten |

| *crystal growth from a crucible* | *trimming* | *wafer sawing* | *phosphorous diffusion* | *screen-printing of contacts* | *solar cell* | *string formation* |

Fertigungsprozess eines monokristallinen Moduls
Stages in the production of a monocrystalline module

Solarzellen

Solarzellen werden schon seit Ende der 1950er Jahre in der Raumfahrt und Satellitentechnik eingesetzt und seither stetig weiterentwickelt. Das Kernelement von Solarzellen wird aus einem p-n-Übergang gebildet. Solarzellen bestehen also aus zwei unterschiedlich dotierten Halbleiterschichten. Als Halbleiter werden beispielsweise mono- oder polykristallines Silizium (Si), amorphes Silizium (a-Si), Kadmium–Tellurid (CdTe), oder Kupfer-Indium-Diselenid (CuInSe2), auch CIS genannt, verwendet. Im Falle von CdTe und CIS werden die aktiven p-dotierten CdTe- bzw. CIS-Schichten zur Herstellung eines p-n-Überganges mit n-dotierten Kadmiumsulfid-Schichten (CdS) bedeckt. Diese Dioden werden auch „Heterodioden" genannt, da verschiedene Halbleiter in einer Zelle eingesetzt werden. Silizium-Solarzellen bestehen nur aus (n- und p-dotiertem) Silizium.

Solarzellen werden in der Regel als Scheiben oder Schichten erzeugt. Der p-n-Übergang liegt parallel zur Oberfläche. Durch Absorption der einfallenden Photonen werden im Halbleiter Ladungsträger freigesetzt, die durch das elektrische Feld des p-n-Übergangs bewegt werden und einen Strom erzeugen können. Metallische Kontakte führen den Strom zum Verbraucher. Damit das Licht, das auf die Oberfläche auftrifft, in den Halbleiter eindringen

kann, bestehen die dem Licht zugewandten Kontakte meist aus schmalen **Leiterbahnen** oder transparenten leitfähigen Schichten. Auf der Zellrückseite befindet sich eine durchgehende leitende Metallschicht, da hier kein Licht auftrifft.

Der gebräuchlichste Halbleiter, der bei Solarzellen Verwendung findet, ist **Silizium**. Bei der Produktion gibt es drei unterschiedliche Verfahren, aus denen drei verschiedene Zelltypen hervorgehen: monokristalline, polykristalline (auch multikristalline genannt) und amorphe. Bei monokristallinen Zellen wird der Siliziumbruch geschmolzen und daraus bei einer Temperatur von ca. 1400°C ein zylinderförmiger Silizium-Einkristall mit einem Durchmesser von ungefähr 15 cm gezogen, der anschließend in 0,2 bis 0,4 mm dünne Scheiben (engl.: *wafer*) gesägt wird; aus diesen werden in der Regel Rechtecke mit Kantenlängen von 10 bis 15 cm geschnitten, aber auch unbeschnittene runde Zellen sind üblich. Für polykristalline Zellen lässt man die Schmelze in Gießformen zu einem rechteckigen Kristallblock erstarren. Dann werden ebenfalls *wafer* hergestellt. Beim Abkühlungsprozess entstehen unterschiedlich große Kristallite. Durch das Einbringen von Fremdatomen bei 800°C werden die genannten p-n-Übergänge in den Scheiben erzeugt.

Monokristalline Siliziumzellen haben ein gleichmäßigeres Farbbild als polykristalline, die durch den Erstarrungsvorgang ihr etwas unruhigeres Erscheinungsbild erhalten. Amorphes Silizium (wie auch CdTe und CIS) wird in dünnen Schichten auf ein Trägermaterial aufgedampft oder abgeschieden.

Auf der Vorderseite der Zellen befinden sich das Gitter aus Leiterbahnen sowie eine **Antireflexschicht**. Diese wenige 100 nm dünne Schicht reduziert wie im photographischen Objektiv die Lichtreflexion und erhöht somit die Energieausbeute. Die Antireflexschicht ist so gestaltet, dass die Reflexion von Photonen aus dem roten Spektralbereich (für den die Zelle am empfindlichsten ist) minimiert wird. Als Folge der weniger reduzierten Reflexion des blauen Lichtes ergibt sich für die Zelle der bekannte dunkelblaue bis schwarze Farbton. Durch Variation der Schichtdicke können auch Zellen anderer Farben, zum Beispiel Magenta (rötlich) oder Gold (gelblich), erzeugt werden, allerdings mit der Konsequenz geringerer Lichtausbeute.

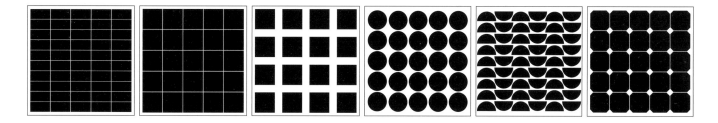

Schematische Darstellung der möglichen Anordnung poly- und monokristalliner Zellen (Auswahl)
Schematic diagram of possible arrangements of poly- und monocrystalline cells (selection)

Solar Cells

Solar cells have been employed since the end of the 1950s to provide electric power to space ships and satellites and have been steadily developed further.

The core element of solar cells is, as described before, a p-n junction. Solar cells thus consist of two differently doped semiconductor layers. The following semiconductors are used today: mono- and polycrystalline silicon (Si), amorphous silicon (a-Si), cadmium-telluride (CdTe), or copper-indium-diselenide (CuInSe2) also called CIS.

In the cases of CdTe and CIS, the active, positively doped CdTe and CIS films respectively are covered by negatively doped cadmium-sulfide (CdS) films in order to obtain p-n junctions. Such diodes are called "heterodiodes" as different semiconductors are employed in one cell. Silicon solar cells consist only of (n- and p-doped) silicon.

As a rule, solar cells are made in the form of discs or films. The p-n junction is positioned parallel to the surface. By the absorption of incoming photons, charge carriers are liberated, which are moved by the built-in electric field of the p-n junction, forming an electric current. Metal contacts transport the current to the consumer. In order to enable light incident onto the surface to enter the semiconductor, the contacts on the light-facing side of the cell generally consist of narrow, comb-like **conductor stripes** or transparent conductive layers. At the back of the cells, where no light enters, a homogeneous metal layer is deposited.

The semiconductor most widely employed for making solar cells is **silicon**. Three different techniques are used, leading to three different types of solar cells: monocrystalline, polycrystalline and amorphous. In the case of monocrystalline cells, broken, pre-cleaned silicon is molten and at 1400°C a cylindrical single crystal of 15 to 20 cm^2 diameter grows, starting with a small nucleus. This crystal is subsequently sawn into 0.2 to 0.3 mm thick discs ("wafers"). Out of these round wafers, typically squares of 10 to 15 cm length are cut. In some cases the more material-economic round wafers are used. To obtain polycrystalline (also called "multicrystalline") cells, silicon is molten in rectangular crucibles. Upon solidification, rectangular crystal blocks are obtained (and later also cut into wafers). Under these conditions generally crystallites of different sizes are forming the solid material. The p-n junctions are generated by in-diffusion of doping atoms (typically phosphorous) at 800°C.

Monocrystalline silicon cells show a more homogeneous colour than polycrystalline cells, which get a more varied appearance by the process of solidification. Amorphous silicon cells as well as those of CdTe and CIS are produced by the deposition of thin films on a suitable carrier material (substrate).

On the front surface of the cells, the aforementioned grid of conductor stripes is deposited and, in addition, an **antireflection layer**. This antireflection layer, which is only a few hundred nm thick, reduces light reflection - like in photographic lenses - and thus enhances the efficiency of light utilisation. This layer is adjusted via its thickness so that the reflection of light from the red spectral region (for which the cell shows highest sensitivity) is minimised. As the reflection of blue light is less reduced, the cells show the well-known blue to black appearance. By variation of the thickness of the antireflection coating different colours can be obtained, for example magenta (reddish) or golden (yellow) – causing, however, a lower light use.

Photovoltaik-Module

Bei den auf dem Markt erhältlichen Standardmodulen handelt es sich hauptsächlich um **kristalline Silizium-Module**. Eine neuere Entwicklung stellen **Dünnschichtmodule** dar. Um ein breites Strahlungsspektrum nutzen zu können, wird außerdem mit **Tandem- oder Stapelzellen** experimentiert, bei denen unterschiedliche Halbleitermaterialien, die sich für die Nutzung verschiedener Spektralbereiche des Sonnenlichts eignen, übereinander angeordnet werden.

Photovoltaik-Module bestehen aus elektrisch verbundenen Solarzellen, die zum Schutz gegen äußere Einflüsse (mechanische Beanspruchung, Witterung, Korrosion) zwischen geeigneten Materialien, meist Glas, eingebettet und mit transparenten Kunststoffen versiegelt sind. Der Mindestabstand der Zellen voneinander beträgt bei Modulen aus kristallinem Silizium 2 mm; Standardmodule haben meist einen Zellabstand von 2–5 mm. Bei Dünnschichtmodulen haben die durchschnittlich einen Zentimeter breiten Zellen einen kaum wahrnehmbaren Abstand von ca. 0,5 mm.

Typische Spannungswerte einer Siliziumzelle liegen zwischen 0,5 und 0,8 V. Da eine Spannung von 0,5 V für technische Anwendungen zu niedrig ist, wird eine höhere Spannung durch die Serienverschaltung mehrerer Einzelzellen erreicht. Bei einer **Parallelschaltung** addiert sich der Strom der Zellen bei gleichbleibender Spannung, **Reihenschaltung** bewirkt eine Addition der Spannung bei gleichbleibendem Strom. Üblich sind kristalline Module mit 36, 72 oder 144 Zellen mit Spannungen von 20 bis 70 V.

Dünnschichtmodule werden aus neuen Halbleitern wie amorphem Silizium, Kupfer-Indium-Diselenid (CIS) oder Kadmium-Tellurid (CdTe) hergestellt. In automatisierten Verfahren werden Einzelzellen in Schichten direkt ohne sichtbare Leiterbänder auf ein Trägermaterial (**Substrat**) aufgebracht. Dies führt zu einem gleichmäßigeren Erscheinungsbild als bei kristallinen Modulen. Durch geeignete Strukturierung der Teilschichten (Kontaktschichten und Halbleiterschichten) können direkt ohne Lötvorgänge integriert verschaltete Module hergestellt werden, die typischerweise 100 einzelne, seriell verbundene Zellen enthalten. In der Dünnschichttechnologie ergibt der Produktionsprozess immer ein fertiges Modul. Üblich sind Maße von 60 cm x 120 cm, aber auch die Produktion kleinerer oder größerer Module ist prinzipiell möglich. Ihre Farbe ist in der Regel Schwarz, seltener Dunkelgrün oder Dunkelbraun.

Um die miteinander verschalteten Solarzellen für die Dauer ihrer Nutzung vor Umwelteinflüssen zu schützen und die elektrisch einwandfreie Funktion zu gewährleisten, werden die Zellen mit geeigneten Materialien (Rück- und Vorderseite) zu einem Verbund zusammengefügt. Bei kristallinen Zellen geschieht dies mit Gießharz oder zwischen zwei Folien unter Druck und hoher Temperatur, wobei die vordere und hintere Modulabdeckung aus Glas, Acrylglas oder Folie bestehen können. Auch bei Dünnschichtmodulen werden als Substrat meist Glas oder ein flexibles, hitzebeständiges Material wie Metall und für die Vorderseite Glas oder Folie verwendet. Während bei CIS-Modulen hochtransparentes eisenarmes Weißglas für die Vorderseite verwendet wird, um hohe Lichtdurchlässigkeit zu gewährleisten, genügt bei CdTe-Modulen billigeres klassisches Fensterglas (Natron-Kalk-Glas). Die verschiedenen Schichten werden mit Kunststoff hermetisch versiegelt.

Ein Glas/Glas-Modul ist eine Verbundverglasung, bei der die eingesetzte Folie die Eigenstabilität bei Glasbruch sichert. Deshalb kann es direkt in Isolier- oder Überkopfverglasungen, die aus thermischen oder sicherheitstechnischen Gründen immer aus mehreren Scheiben bestehen müssen, eingesetzt werden. Allerdings besitzt nur Verbundglas mit PVB (Poly-Vinyl-Butyral) die grundsätzliche Genehmigung als Überkopfverglasung. Für mit EVA (Ethyl-Vinyl-Azetat) laminierte Module wird jedoch von den Behörden in der Regel eine Einzelgenehmigung erteilt.

Standardmodule sind im Allgemeinen gerahmt, die meisten Hersteller bieten aber auch rahmenlose Module an. Der Rahmen erhöht die Abdichtung des Modulverbundes und schützt die Modulkanten, stellt aber einen zusätzlichen Preisfaktor dar. Der elektrische Anschluss wird mit einer auf der Rückseite angebrachten Kunststoffdose und speziell ausgelegten Kabeln sowie spritzwassergeschützten Steckern oder einer in den Rahmen integrierten Lösung realisiert. Aus gestalterischen oder baulichen Gründen ist es zur besseren Integration der Module, beispielsweise in Fassadenkonstruktionen, oft sinnvoll, auf rahmenlose Module zurückzugreifen.

1   Rahmen
Frame

2   Weißglas
Flint glass

3 + 5   Transparente Laminierungsfolie
Transparent lamination foil

4   Zellenverbund
String formation of cells

6   Laminierungsfolie (transparent oder farbig)
Lamination foil (transparent or coloured)

7   Glas
Glass

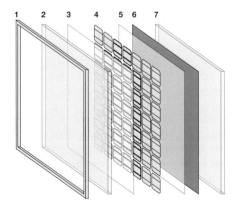

Aufbau eines kristallinen Solarmoduls
Assembly of a silicon solar module

Photovoltaic Modules

The most common standard modules are based on **crystalline silicon cells**. A more recent development is **thin-film modules**. In order to efficiently use a wider spectral range of light, experimental studies are underway, which use **"tandem" or "stacked" cells**, in which different semiconductor materials are positioned on top of each other, using different spectral parts of solar radiation.

Photovoltaic modules consist of electrically connected solar cells, which, in order to protect them from harmful environmental influences (mechanical wear, weather conditions, corrosion) are sealed between suitable materials, mostly glass, using transparent plastic sheets as "glue". The minimal distance between cells in crystalline silicon modules is 2 mm; standard modules show cell separations of 2 to 5 mm. Thin-film modules, consisting of cells which are mostly 1 cm wide, have barely visible interspaces of approximately 0.5 mm.

Silicon cells typically exhibit voltages between 0.5 and 0.8 V. As such low voltages are not desired for practical applications, higher voltages are obtained by series connection of cells. **Parallel connection** leads to addition of the currents of the cells at the same voltage, whereas **series connection** leads to addition of the voltages of the cells. Usually crystalline silicon modules are manufactured having 36, 72 or 144 cells at voltages of 20 to 70 V.

Thin-film modules are made of new semiconductors, such as amorphous silicon, copper-indium-diselenide (CIS) or cadmium-telluride (CdTe). In automated processes individual cell structures are deposited as films on top of each other and are connected serially and directly without visible contacts onto suitable **substrates**, such as glass. This leads to a significantly more homogeneous appearance than observed in crystalline modules. By suitable structuring of the different films forming the cells, integrated connected modules are produced right away, containing typically 100 serially connected cells. Thin-film technology leads directly to complete modules. Usual module sizes are 60 cm x 120 cm, but the production of smaller or larger modules is also feasible. Typically, the colour appearance of thin-film modules is black, in some cases dark green or dark brown.

In order to protect the system of interconnected solar cells for their lifetime from environmental influences and guarantee their proper operation for a long time, the cells are joined with suitable materials (back and front) forming a compound system. In the case of crystalline cells, this is accomplished by resins or plastic sheets under pressure and at elevated temperatures; the covers can be glass, acrylic glass or foils. In the case of thin-film modules, glass or a heat resistant material, such as a metal sheet, are used for the back and glass or foils at the front. Whereas for CIS-modules highly transparent iron-poor white glass is used, for CdTe-modules a standard window pane glass (sodium-lime glass) is sufficient. The different layers are hermetically sealed with plastic.

A glass/glass module is de facto a compound or laminated glass, in which the included plastic sheet guarantees stability upon breakage. It can be therefore used directly in insulation or overhead glazing, which generally require a multi-glass pane for thermal and safety reasons. Only laminated glass using PVB (poly-vinyl-butyral) has the basic permission for such use in overhead glazing. For modules using EVA (ethyl-vinyl-acetate) a single permit is usually obtained from the authorities.

Standard modules are generally offered with frames, but most manufacturers also offer frameless modules. A frame improves sealing of the module and also protects the edges from breakage, but implies higher costs. The electrical connection is obtained via integrated contact boxes at the rear, special cables and water-protected plugs. For design and construction-related reasons, for example in façade installations, it is often recommendable to use frameless modules.

Aufbringen einer Molybdänschicht auf Fensterglas	Strukturieren des Rückkontaktes per Laserstrahl	Beschichten mit Kupfer-Indium-Diselenid (CIS)	Abscheiden einer Puffer-Schicht aus Kadmiumsulfid	Strukturieren durch mechanisches Ritzen	Auftragen einer leitenden Zinkoxid-Schicht	Strukturieren durch mechanisches Ritzen	Verkapseln mit Deckglas

Deposition of a molybdenum film on glass	*Laser structuring of the back side contact*	*Deposition of copper-indium-diselenide (CIS)*	*Deposition of a cadmium-sulfide buffer layer*	*Structuring by mechanical scribing*	*Deposition of a conducting zinc-oxide film*	*Structuring by mechanical scribing*	*Sealing with a cover glass*

Fertigungsprozess eines CIS-Dünnschichtmoduls

Stages in the production of a CIS thin-film module

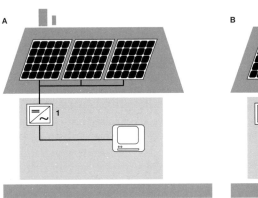

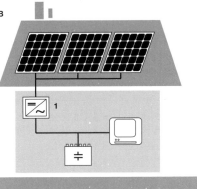

A Der Strom wird sofort verbraucht
The current is consumed directly

B Speichern des (überschüssigen) Stroms in einer Batterie
The (surplus) current is stored in a battery

1 Wechselrichter
Inverter

Systemkonzepte
System concepts

Photovoltaik-Anlagen

Grundsätzlich gibt es zwei unterschiedliche Anlagentypen: Zum einen **Inselsysteme**, die unabhängig vom Stromnetz sind und, um ganzjährig eine autarke Stromversorgung zu garantieren, Speichersysteme zur Gewährleistung der Versorgungssicherheit bei schwankendem Energieertrag benötigen; geeignete Speichersysteme sind Akkumulatoren, Batterien oder ein *back-up*-Generator inklusive Zubehör wie Laderegler zur Spannungsüberwachung der Batterien. Zum anderen gibt es **netzgekoppelte Systeme**, die den Strom in das vorhandene Stromnetz einspeisen bzw. bei Bedarf aus dem Netz entnehmen und so Produktionsschwankungen ausgleichen können; sie müssen mit einem Netzüberwachungsmodul zur störungsfreien Kopplung an das öffentliche Netz ausgestattet sein sowie mit Stromkreisverteilern und Stromzählern zur Ermittlung der Kosten bzw. Vergütungen.

Abgesehen von den genannten spezifischen Komponenten der beiden unterschiedlichen Anlagentypen sind übliche Elemente aller Photovoltaikanlagen die folgenden: Wechselrichter sowie Schaltvorrichtungen, insbesondere Freischalter für Servicearbeiten, da die Module bei Sonneneinfall immer Spannung liefern, Notabschaltungsvorrichtungen für den Brandfall, Leitungen, Sicherungen, Blitzschutzeinrichtungen etc.

Neben den Modulen ist der **Wechselrichter** die wichtigste Systemkomponente; er wandelt den erzeugten Gleichstrom in Wechselstrom (50 Hz, 220 V) um, damit er im Haushalt genutzt oder in das Stromnetz eingespeist werden kann. Der Wechselrichter muss an die installierte Generatorenleistung angepasst werden. Ein **zentraler Wechselrichter** wird bei einer gleichmäßigen Bestrahlung der gesamten Modulfläche gewählt; **dezentrale Wechselrichter** sind modular addierbar und dann zu empfehlen, wenn Modulflächen mit unterschiedlichen Einstrahlungswerten (zum Beispiel durch unterschiedliche Ausrichtung) zusammengeschaltet sind, oder wenn die Erweiterbarkeit der Anlage gewährleistet werden soll. Wechselrichter sollten an einem kühlen, geschützten Ort installiert werden, da sie ca. 2 bis 5 Prozent der Leistung als Verlustwärme freisetzen.

Was die **Auslegung der Anlagen** angeht, so wird die Größe eines **Inselsystems** vor allem durch den durchschnittlichen Strombedarf, den Nutzungszeitraum und die Bedarfsspitzen bestimmt. Die Anlage muss so ausgelegt sein, dass auch in Zeiten des höchsten Bedarfs die Versorgung gewährleistet ist. Versorgungssicherheit ermöglicht ein Energiemanagement, das starke Stromverbraucher (zum Beispiel eine Waschmaschine) nur bei hoher Solarstromproduktion (also um die Mittagszeit) eintaktet. Ein solches Energiemanagement und der Einsatz sparsamer Stromverbraucher reduzieren die notwendige Größe der Anlage. Bei **netzgekoppelten Systemen** wird die Größe eher durch die geeignete Fläche und das verfügbare Investitionskapital vorgegeben. Das Energiemanagement liegt hier beim Netzbetreiber, der mit dem überschüssigen Solarstrom Bedarfsspitzen anderer Kunden abfängt. Für Gewerbenutzungen ist der Einsatz von Photovoltaik besonders geeignet, da Bedarfs- und Solarstrahlungskurve über den Tagesverlauf ähnlich sind, und so zu teuren Spitzenzeiten der Strom preisgünstiger selbst produziert wird. Bei Wohngebäuden sollte mit der Auslegung der Anlage die Deckung des eigenen Strombedarfs bei geringem Energiebezug aus dem Netz erreicht werden. Bedarfsspitzen entstehen bei Wohnnutzungen eher zu Zeiten, an denen die Strahlungskurve niedrig ist (morgens und abends), der Energieüberschuss wird um die Mittagszeit erzeugt. Unter den Bedingungen des derzeitigen Einspeisegesetzes in Deutschland wird üblicherweise der gesamte Solarstrom an das Energieversorgungsunternehmen verkauft, das einen höheren Betrag vergüten muss, als es selbst berechnet. Dies entlastet den Eigentümer der Anlage vom Energiemanagement.

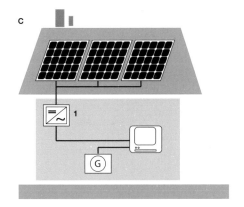

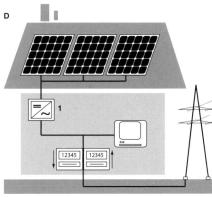

Photovoltaic Plants

There are two different types of photovoltaic facilities: **Island systems** or **stand-alone systems**, which are independent from the power grid and, in order to guarantee continuous power supply over the year at varying yield, require storage or back-up systems. Suitable components are accumulators respectively batteries or back-up generators including power conditioning systems, like charge-controllers for batteries.

The second type are **grid-connected systems**, which feed their power into the public utilities' grid and take power out of the grid, in order to compensate for output variations. These systems need a surveillance system for coupling to the grid, distribution systems and current counters for determining cost, respectively reimbursement.

Besides the aforementioned specific and differing components of both systems, the following elements are required in all types: inverters, switching systems, especially decoupling switches for service work, as the modules under solar irradiation always deliver a voltage, an automatic turn-off switch in the case of a fire, special cables (suited for dc electricity), suitable fuses and lightning protection.

Besides the modules, the **inverter** is the most important system component. It changes the direct current produced by the modules into alternating current at 50 Hz and 220V for direct use in standard appliances or to feed it into the grid. It has to be adapted to the installed power level. A **central inverter** is used under homogeneous irradiation of the total module area. **De-central inverters** can be added and are suitable if different parts of the module area are experiencing different irradiation profiles (e.g. by different orientations to the sun), or to allow addition of further modules. Inverters should be positioned in a cool, well ventilated place, as they emit 2 to 5 percent of the generator power as waste heat.

Regarding the **layout of the plant**, the size of an **island system** is determined by the average power demand, the time of usage and peak demand. The plant should be designed so that it can guarantee supply even in times of maximum demand. Safety of supply can be improved by an energy management system, which switches on large consumers (like washing machines) only at times of high supply (around noon). Such energy management as well as use of economic consumers can significantly reduce the size of the plant. In the case of **grid-connected systems**, the size of a plant will more likely be determined by the available area and capital. The energy buffer is provided by the utility, which can use surplus energy from the photovoltaic plant to cover peak demand of other customers. Photovoltaic power is especially well suited for use in commercial entities, which have peak requirements synchronous with the power production and can shave-off demand on the utility at expensive peak times. In residential buildings peak demand occurs typically at times when the supply is lower (morning and evening) and at noon a surplus is generated. Under conditions of the present reimbursement law in Germany the total photovoltaic power is typically sold to the utility, which reimburses a higher amount than it charges. This makes an energy management system for the facility owner redundant.

Energieausbeute und Ausrichtung

Die Energieausbeute einer Photovoltaikanlage hängt von der geographischen Lage, der Sonnenscheindauer und dem Einstrahlungswinkel der Sonne ab. Sie wird als Jahresertrag in kWh/m² ermittelt.

Um **maximalen Energieertrag** zu erzielen, sollten die Module möglichst günstig zur Sonne orientiert sein, deren Bewegung im Tagesverlauf jedoch einen gewissen Spielraum zulässt. Optimal für Mitteleuropa ist eine Ausrichtung nach Süden mit einer Neigung von 30 bis 35 Grad gegen die Horizontale. Aber auch ein nach Süden ausgerichtetes, vertikal angebrachtes Modul oder ein ideal geneigtes, nach Osten oder Westen orientiertes Modul erbringt immer noch eine Energieausbeute von 75 Prozent des Optimums.

Wichtig ist auch, dass die Modulflächen so geplant werden, dass sie im Tagesverlauf nicht durch Bäume, Nachbargebäude oder die Gebäudegeometrie selbst (Dachüberstände, Gesimse, Erker etc. bei Anbringung an Fassaden, Schornsteine und dergleichen bei Dachmontage) verschattet werden. Gering erscheinende Verschattungen können unter Umständen die gesamte Anlage zum Ausfall bringen, da eine verschattete Zelle einen hohen elektrischen Widerstand im System darstellt.

Modul- und Leistungsdaten

Der **Wirkungsgrad** bezeichnet, welchen Anteil der Sonnenstrahlung eine Solarzelle in elektrische Leistung umsetzen kann, und wird in Prozent ausgedrückt. Ein Teil der Energie wird in Wärme umgesetzt und geht für die elektrische Energieumwandlung verloren. Dies führt zu einer Aufheizung der Module auf typischerweise 60°C. Theoretisch ist maximal ein Wirkungsgrad von 43 Prozent möglich, im Labor hat man bereits Werte um 23 Prozent erzielt. In der Praxis werden zwar allgemein geringere Werte erreicht, an einer Steigerung wird aber in der Entwicklung stetig gearbeitet. Monokristalline Siliziummodule haben derzeit einen Wirkungsgrad von 14 bis 17 Prozent, polykristalline von 13 bis 15 Prozent, amorphe hingegen lediglich

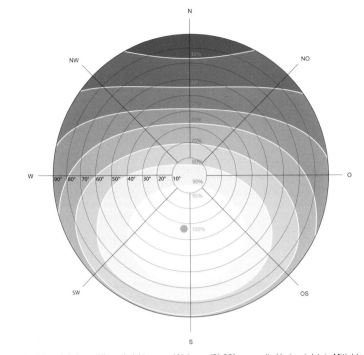

Energieertrag in Abhängigkeit von Himmelsrichtung und Neigung (0°-90° gegen die Horizontale) in Mitteldeutschland
Energy yield in relation to orientation and inclination (0°-90° towards the horizontal line) in central Germany

von 5 bis 7 Prozent. Dünnschichtzellen besitzen einen Wirkungsgrad von nur ca. 8 Prozent, verbrauchen aber wesentlich weniger Material und sind deshalb und auch wegen des einfacheren Herstellungsprozesses preiswerter. (Der Preis wird in Euro pro W_p angegeben.) Praktisch bedeutet ein Wirkungsgrad von 10 Prozent, dass 1 m² Modulfläche bei senkrechtem Lichteinfall eine elektrische Leistung von 100 W (Watt) erzeugt.

Ein photovoltaisches System wird durch seine **Spitzenleistung** in „Watt peak" (W_p) charakterisiert. Diese **Nennleistung** gibt das Modul bei direkter, senkrechter Sonneneinstrahlung einer Intensität von 1000 W/m² und einem definierten Sonnenspektrum (AM 1,5) bei einer Zelltemperatur von 25°C ab. Ein Modul hat typischerweise eine Leistung von 10 bis 100 W_p. Je nach Zell- bzw. Modultyp benötigt eine Anlage mit 1 kWp Leistung eine Fläche von 9 bis 20 m².

Die **Performance Ratio** (PR) gibt den Ertrag eines Systems an im Verhältnis zum Ertrag eines idealen, verlustfreien Systems mit gleicher Auslegung, Nennleistung und Ortsangabe. Sie spiegelt die Energieeffizienz aller Komponenten wider, das heißt, sie ist beeinflusst vom Zusammenspiel von Modul und Wechselrichter, Verkabelung und anderen Systemkomponenten, aber unabhängig von Wirkungsgrad und Ausrichtung der Module. Die PR liegt bei modernen Anlagen bei 0,7 bis 0,8. Eine PR von 0,8 etwa bedeutet, dass das System 20 Prozent Ertrag „verschenkt". Verschattung und Verschmutzung, aber auch steigende Modultemperatur bewirken eine Minderung der Leistung. Derzeitige Wechselrichter weisen Verluste von unter 5 Prozent auf.

Energy Yield and Orientation

The energy yield of a photovoltaic plant depends primarily on the geographic location, the irradiation duration and the incident angle of the solar radiation. It is determined as an annual yield in kWh/m^2.

To achieve a **maximum yield** the modules should be oriented at an optimal angle to the sun, although the movement of the sun during the day allows for a certain degree of flexibility. For central Europe a southern orientation at an angle of 30 to 35 degrees to the horizontal level is optimal. But a module oriented vertically to the ground or oriented at the ideal angle towards the east or west still delivers 75 percent of the optimum value.

It is very important that a photovoltaic plant is constructed in such a way that it is not shaded by trees, neighbouring buildings, or the geometric aspects of the building that carries it (roof projections, mouldings, bay-windows etc. with regard to façade-mounted systems, or chimneys and the like with regard to roof-mounted systems). Apparently low shading can bring down the whole installation, as a shaded cell represents a high electric resistance in the system.

Module and Performance Data

The concept of **efficiency** signifies the amount of electric output of the module or cell in relation to the total radiation input and is given as a percentage. A part of the incoming radiation is converted into thermal energy and lost for electricity production. This leads to a heat-up of modules to temperatures of typically 60 percent. Theoretical values of efficiency are around 43 percent. Best laboratory values have been 23 percent, by using elaborate concepts. Values of commercial products are definitely lower, but work is in progress to improve the performance. Monocrystalline silicon modules presently show efficiencies of 14 to 17 percent, polycrystalline modules show 13 to 15 percent, amorphous modules deliver only 5 to 7 percent. Present thin-film modules have efficiencies of only 8 percent, but they use less material and are cheaper to manufacture in integrated factories and can thus compete with silicon in specific price, given in Euro per W$_p$. As a guideline, an efficiency of 10 percent means that a module of 1 m^2 under vertical irradiation at a clear sunny day delivers an electric power of 100 W.

A photovoltaic system is characterised by its **peak power** given in W$_p$ (watt peak). This **nominal power** is the power which the module delivers under direct, vertical solar irradiation at an intensity of 1000 W/m^2, a defined solar spectrum (AM 1,5) and a cell temperature of 25°C. A typical module has a nominal power of 10 to 100 W$_p$. Depending on the cell respectively module type a photovoltaic installation of a nominal power of 1 kW$_p$ requires an area of 9 to 20 m^2.

Another characteristic rating is given by the **performance ratio** (PR), meaning the yield of the system considered in relation to an ideally designed, loss-free system of the same layout, nominal power and location. This value reflects the energy efficiency of all components and is influenced by the cooperation of modules, inverter, wiring and other system components, but independent of efficiency and orientation of the modules. The PR of modern plants lies at 0.7 to 0.8. A PR of 0.8 means, for example, that the system wastes 20 percent of electrical energy. Shading and dirt, but also high module temperature (caused by low cooling efficiency) lead to lower yields. State-of-the-art inverters have losses of less than 5 percent.

Rechnerische Ermittlung einer Verschattung
Calculated value of shadowing

1 Sonnentiefststand 21. Dezember
Winter solstice 21st of December

β Winkel des Sonnentiefststandes
Angle of the winter solstice

M Mindestabstand
Minimum distance

H Höhe des Schatten werfenden Objekts
Height of the shadowing object

$$\tan \beta = H/M$$

Beispiel
Example

β = 20°

M = 5 m ->   tan 20° = H/5

max H = tan 20° x 5

max H = 0,364 x 5

max H = 1,82 m

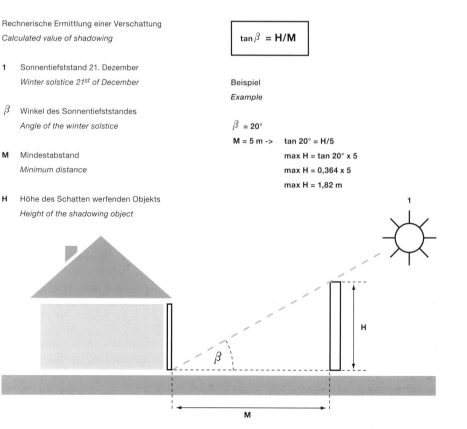

Die **energetische Rücklaufzeit** gibt an, wie lange ein System braucht, um die bei der Herstellung aufgewendete Energie zurückzuliefern. Die Bilanz ist positiv, wenn sie kleiner ist als die Lebensdauer. Bei kristallinen Modulen beträgt sie 3 bis 4 Jahre, bei Dünnschichtmodulen 1 bis 2 Jahre.

Der **Erntefaktor** gibt an, wie oft das System die zu seiner Herstellung benötigte Energie während seiner Lebensdauer wieder einspielt. Bei einer Lebensdauer von 30 Jahren liegt der Erntefaktor für monokristalline Siliziummodule bei 5 bis 8, für polykristalline Siliziummodule bei 7 bis 14 und für Dünnschichtmodule bei 9 bis 21.

Photovoltaikmodule haben eine **Lebensdauer** von mindestens 30 Jahren (ältere Photovoltaikanlagen gibt es bisher noch nicht im Praxistest). Die Hersteller geben deshalb zurzeit eine Leistungsgarantie von 20 bis 25 Jahren, das heißt, es wird garantiert, dass in diesem Zeitraum die Leistung um weniger als 20 Prozent von der Nennleistung abweicht.

Planungshilfen

Es gibt inzwischen zahlreiche Computerprogramme, die zwar nicht den Fachplaner ersetzen, aber als Planungshilfe dienen können. Mit diesen können die folgenden wesentlichen Planungsfaktoren erfasst bzw. geklärt werden: Dimensionierung der Anlage; Simulation von möglichen Verschattungen; Entwicklung der Systemkonfiguration; Analyse des Betriebsverhaltens; Ertragsprognosen; Wirtschaftlichkeitsberechnungen.

Wirtschaftlichkeit

Die Wirtschaftlichkeit von Photovoltaikanlagen ist umso größer, je höher die Vergleichskosten einer netzgebundenen Stromversorgung sind. **Einspeisevergütung** und verfügbare **Fördermittel** sind weitere zu berücksichtigende Faktoren.

In Deutschland beträgt die Einspeisevergütung durch den Energieversorger gemäß dem Erneuerbare-Energien-Gesetz (EEG), das im Jahr 2000 verabschiedet und im Jahr 2004 no-velliert wurde, über 20 Jahre zwischen 54 und 57,4 Cent/kWh, je nach Größe der Anlage. Für an Fassaden installierte Anlagen gibt es einen Extra-Bonus. Die Vergütung liegt jedes Jahr für neue Anlagen um einige Prozent niedriger, da ein Sinken der Kosten erwartet wird, bleibt aber dann für 20 Jahre konstant.

Zahlreiche EU-Länder, darunter Frankreich, Österreich, Portugal und Spanien, haben Einspeisegesetze ähnlich dem deutschen verabschiedet, die auch die Photovoltaik berücksichtigen, oder bereiten entsprechende Regelungen vor, zum Beispiel Italien. Die Garantie, über einen längeren Zeitraum eine bestimmte Rückvergütung zu bekommen, reduziert das Investitionsrisiko und macht die Errichtung von Photovoltaikanlagen auch für Privathaushalte oder mittelständische Betriebe interessant.

Darüber hinaus gibt es in mehreren europäischen Ländern Förderprogramme für Photovoltaikanlagen auf nationaler oder auch regionaler Ebene. In Deutschland wären hier unter anderem die zinsvergünstigten Darlehen der KfW (Kreditanstalt für Wiederaufbau) zu nennen. Da sich die Förderlandschaft jedoch stetig verändert, ist es sinnvoll, sich vor Planung und Bau einer Photovoltaikanlage über die aktuellen Bedingungen zu informieren. Entsprechende Informationsquellen finden sich auch im Internet, etwa unter www.foerderdata.de. Empfehlenswert für allgemeine Informationen und weiterführende Links auf europäischer Ebene ist auch www.iea-pvps.org (IEA = Internationale Energie-Agentur).

Die **durchschnittlichen Kosten** für ca. 10 m^2 Solargeneratorfläche, die ca. 1 kW$_p$ erzeugen, betragen 4500 bis 5500 Euro (netzgekoppelte Anlage, kristalline Module, alle Anlagenkomponenten inklusive). 1 kW$_p$ an einem Standort im Rhein-Main-Gebiet beispielsweise liefert durchschnittlich 850 kWh/a, mit denen in Deutschland derzeit eine Einspeisevergütung von ca. 470 Euro pro Jahr erzielt wird. Auf Einfamilienhäusern werden je nach Dachfläche und verfügbarem Budget im Normalfall Anlagen mit Nennleistungen zwischen 1 und 5 kW$_p$ installiert. Bei einer Lebensdauer von 30 Jahren liegt die **wirtschaftliche Amortisationszeit** einer geförderten Photovoltaikanlage entsprechend den aktuellen Förderbedingungen bei 10 bis 20 Jahren.

Abschließend sollte nochmals darauf hingewiesen werden, dass bei der Kosten-Nutzen-Kalkulation für Photovoltaikanlagen diejenigen Kosteneinsparungen einbezogen werden müssen, die sich ergeben, wenn bei der Gebäudeintegration der Anlagen Materialien (zum Beispiel Dachdeckung) eingespart werden.

The energy **payback time** signifies the time the system (module) needs to return the energy consumed for its manufacture. The balance is positive, if the payback time is less than the lifetime. Crystalline modules today have payback times of 3 to 4 years, thin-film modules of 1 to 2 years.

The **harvest factor** indicates the number of times that the system brings in its manufacturing energy. At a lifetime of 30 years the harvest factor is 5 to 8 for monocrystalline silicon modules, 7 to 14 for polycrystalline silicon modules and 9 to 21 for thin-film modules.

Photovoltaic modules have a **lifetime** of 30 years or more. (There are no comparable older photovoltaic systems.) Manufacturers presently give a performance guarantee of 20 to 25 years, which means they guarantee that the power output will deviate less than 20 percent from the nominal power during that time.

Planning Support Tools

Today there are many computer applications which can help to plan a new system, although they cannot substitute the expert professional planner. The following planning factors can be clarified and determined: Dimension of the plant; Simulation of possible shading; Development of the system configuration; Analysis of the operation conditions; Forecast of yield; Calculation of economic data.

Economics

The profitability of a photovoltaic installation is greater, the higher the comparative cost of a grid-based supply is. **Feed-in rates** and available **funding** are also of importance.

In Germany the feed-in rate to be paid by the utility, determined by the feed-in law (EEG) of 2000 and modified in 2004, is from 54 to 57.4 cents per kWh, depending on the size of the installation. An extra bonus is paid for façade installations. For new installations the rate is decreased each year by a few percent, taking into account the expected decreasing cost of the installation, but after initiation of the plant it stays constant for 20 years.

A number of EC countries have decreed similar laws involving photovoltaic installations, for example France, Austria, Portugal and Spain, or are preparing similar laws, like Italy. The guarantee to obtain a defined reimbursement over 20 years reduces the risk of the investment and makes photovoltaic installations of interest also for private households and small and medium enterprises.

Moreover, in some European countries credit programmes for photovoltaic installations exist. In Germany, among others, the KfW (*Kreditanstalt für Wiederaufbau*) offers low-interest credits. As these programmes change quite often, it is advisable to obtain detailed information on the actual conditions before planning and building a photovoltaic installation. Information can also be obtained on the internet, e.g. under www.foerderdata.de. General information and links on the European level can be found at www.iea-pvps.org (IEA = International Energy Agency).

The average costs of a 10 m² photovoltaic installation, at a nominal power of 1 kWp, presently amount to 4,500 to 5,500 Euro (grid-connected system, crystalline silicon modules and all components included). A 1 kWp system in the Rhein-Main area in Germany for example produces about 850 kWh annually. Considering the presently valid reimbursement rate, approximately 470 Euro per year are obtained from that.

On single homes, depending on roof area and available budget, systems of a nominal power between 1 and 5 kWp are usually being installed. At a lifetime of 30 years the **amortisation time** under the present funding conditions is between 10 and 20 years.

Finally it should be mentioned that in cost-benefit calculations for photovoltaic installations those cost savings have to be considered which result from the saving of other building components, like roof tiles, when the installation is building-integrated.

Abbildungsnachweis

Image Credits

Allen, die durch Überlassung von Photos und Bildvorlagen, durch Erteilung der Reproduktionserlaubnis und durch Informationen zum Zustandekommen des Buches beigetragen haben, sagen die Autorinnen aufrichtigen Dank. Sämtliche Zeichnungen in diesem Buch wurden eigens angefertigt. Nicht gesondert nachgewiesene Photos stammen von den in den Projektbeschreibungen genannten Architekten, Bauherren oder Produktherstellern. Trotz intensiver Bemühungen konnten einige Urheber von Photos oder Abbildungen nicht ermittelt werden. Zur Klärung eventueller Ansprüche bitten wir, sich mit dem Verlag in Verbindung zu setzen.

The authors wish to express their sincere thanks to all those who have contributed to this book by photographs and illustrations, by granting reproduction rights, and by providing relevant information. All drawings and illustrations were specifically produced for this book. The copyright of photographs which are not listed separately belong to those architects, building owners or system providers named in the project descriptions. Despite intensive efforts it was not possible to identify all the holders of the illustration copyrights. Should a specific copy right be trespassed upon, please address the publisher for its clearing.

6. July ,06   Eastern 16. '75   94334